# Using the **Parallel Curriculum Model** in **Urban Settings**

## Grades K–8

**Sandra N. Kaplan** | **Irene Guzman** | **Carol Ann Tomlinson**

CORWIN
A SAGE Company

Copyright © 2009 by Corwin

*For information:*

Corwin
A SAGE Company
2455 Teller Road
Thousand Oaks, California 91320
(800) 233-9936
Fax: (800) 417-2466
www.corwinpress.com

SAGE Ltd.
1 Oliver's Yard
55 City Road
London EC1Y 1SP
United Kingdom

SAGE India Pvt. Ltd.
B 1/I 1 Mohan Cooperative Industrial Area
Mathura Road, New Delhi 110 044
India

SAGE Asia-Pacific Pte. Ltd.
33 Pekin Street #02-01
Far East Square
Singapore 048763

Printed in the United States of America

*Library of Congress Cataloging-in-Publication Data*

Kaplan, Sandra N.
Using the parallel curriculum model in urban settings, grades K–8/Sandra N. Kaplan, Irene Guzman, and Carol Ann Tomlinson.
    p. cm.
Includes bibliographical references and index.
ISBN 978-1-4129-7218-5 (cloth: alk. paper)
ISBN 978-1-4129-7219-2 (pbk.: alk. paper)
    1. Curriculum planning. 2. Education, Urban. 3. Education, Primary. I. Guzman, Irene. II. Tomlinson, Carol A. III. Title.

LB2806.15.K37 2009
372.19—dc22                              2009031803

This book is printed on acid-free paper.

09  10  11  12  13   10  9  8  7  6  5  4  3  2  1

| | |
|---|---|
| *Acquisitions Editor:* | David Chao |
| *Editorial Assistant:* | Brynn Saito |
| *Production and Copy Editor:* | Jane Haenel |
| *Typesetter:* | C&M Digitals (P) Ltd. |
| *Proofreader:* | Susan Schon |
| *Indexer:* | Molly Hall |
| *Cover and Graphic Designer:* | Rose Storey |

# Contents

Additional materials and resources related to
*Using the Parallel Curriculum Model in Urban Settings, Grades K–8*
can be found at www.CorwinPress.com/kaplancurric_resources

# Preface

## *Bridging the Gap*

The purpose of this Preface for educators is synonymous with the purpose of this book for students: to bridge the gap between rhetoric and practice, between the ideal and the real opportunities to develop as scholars in the classroom, and between the demand for achievement and the preparation to become achievers. For educators, the Preface is a simulated scaffolding or the prerequisite knowledge that mediates the teacher's abilities to use the text to attain the goals for which it was written. The first goal is to comprehend the dimensions and value of the parallel curriculum design. The second goal is to implement the parallel curriculum such that culturally, linguistically, economically, and academically diverse urban students learn to become learners—students who understand the role of a student and assume the responsibility to portray the attributes defined by this role in the context of lessons in the classroom.

## BACKGROUND KNOWLEDGE

The Parallel Curriculum Model introduces four types of curricular experiences to students:

1. A review of the standards-based, regular, or basic curriculum—Core Curriculum

2. An introduction to the study of the topics and disciplines—Curriculum of Practice

3. The ability to develop continuity of the curricular experiences—Curriculum of Connections

4. The chance to develop self-understanding—Curriculum of Identity

Each of these curriculums has a distinctive purpose and contributes to an articulated and cohesive plan for teaching and learning.

In this text, the Curriculum of Identity is the predominant contributor to the goals articulated for urban students; it assists diverse students in learning how to learn and to become socialized to school processes so that they acquire access to and equity in the curriculum and instruction provided to them. Pipher, in her book *The Middle of Everywhere* (2002), discusses how students who are new to the country and culturally, economically, linguistically, and academically diverse need to form their identity. She states that this identity is learned in varied contexts by asking questions such as "Who am I?" "What do I want?" "How am I like and/or different from other people?" and "Am I talented?" (p. 319). Being able to identify oneself as a learner is the basis for entering into and retaining one's involvement in the teaching/learning process.

The Curriculum of Identity also affords students the time to internalize their role as student and scholar. The other three parallel curriculums provide situations for introducing, applying, and reinforcing the skills related to developing an identity as a learner. In his book *Race, Culture and Schooling* (2007), Murrell states that "there are aspects of the school's social and cultural environment that are within our control so that children do not feel that they are giving up something to be smart." Murrell asserts that urban teachers can further the development of an identity of achievement for students by facilitating their sense of efficacy in the academic tasks they undertake. The Curriculum of Identity provides the forum to practice and demonstrate the skills needed to build self-efficacy as a learner: developing clarity of the task, becoming curious, challenging ideas, and engaging in the intellectual struggle. These skills shift the control and responsibility for learning to the student, who understands and acknowledges the role of being a learner in different contexts.

Conventional wisdom influences much of what educators learn and subsequently put into their classroom practice. This knowledge often needs to be reinforced and/or augmented by the works of prominent researchers and authors. Discussions concerning why some students of diversity have difficulty learning in school abound with suggestions for analyzing and ameliorating the problem. The concept of intellectual engagement and how it is taught and sustained are consistently addressed as potential solutions to this issue. C. Suarez-Orozco, M. Suarez-Orozco, and I. Todorova in their book *Learning in a New Land* (2008) provide a framework for guiding the curricular and instructional decisions teachers make in developing intellectual engagement. They define Cognitive Engagement, Relational Engagement, and Behavioral Engagement as categorical referents to promote intellectual success. Within these areas of engagement are teaching/learning experiences that develop attitudes toward school, academic self-efficacy, and emotional well-being (pp. 42–54). The lessons in this text have been designed specifically for teachers who wish to accomplish these types of goals.

Educators using the various lessons in this book need to be aware of the principles of learning that both advance and disable students' achievement. Principles such as stating the objective, demonstrating, practicing in differing contexts, rendering feedback, and providing transfer are essential. In the work that has been done with students of diversity in the urban centers, a "bridge" is used to scaffold the students' learning from not knowing to knowing by using simple to complex and concrete to abstract teaching and learning strategies (see the following figure).

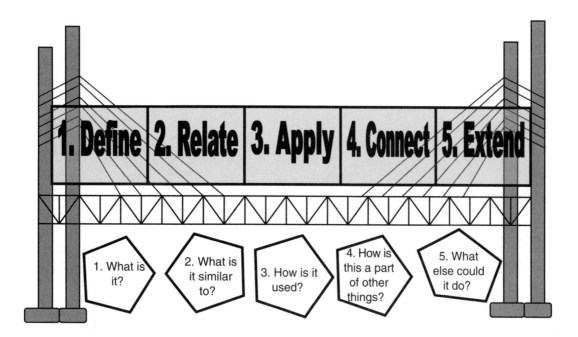

Example: Scaffolding the Skill of Questioning

Skill: Questioning

| 1. Define | 2. Relate | 3. Apply | 4. Connect | 5. Extend |
|-----------|-----------|----------|------------|-----------|
| Request information. | Think about a time when you were curious about something. What kinds of questions did you ask? | Categorize different types of questions: open-ended and closed-ended questions. | Read about a current event. Ask students to think about the questions a journalist had to ask to write the article. | Think about the work of a historian, biologist, or sociologist. What types of questions would they ask in their fields? |

As stated in the body of the text, the lessons here have been divided into segments so that they can be taught incrementally and over time. Any one lesson presented in the text can be taught as a unit of study that takes affect over a designated time frame.

# Acknowledgments

There are seldom enough "thank yous" for all the people that have contributed to the development of any one text. However, there are specific people who helped us understand what urban students need and helped us realize how the implementation of the lessons matched our perceived goals.

We thank Adrienne Hall for her tireless typing and searching for images.

We thank Jessica Manzone for her willingness to "do anything" to be of assistance.

We thank Jessica Tyerman, Pam Lovett, Michelle McGuire, Kim Dodds, and Robert Grubb for their preparation and demonstration of the lessons with urban students during the University of Southern California Teacher Institute and Demonstration School.

We thank the Project Teachers participating in the Javits Grant: Using Models of Teaching to Improve Student Achievement (S206A040072) for their willingness to discuss with us some of their concerns regarding urban students and their needs.

We thank the California Association for the Gifted and the Orange County Council for the Gifted for allowing us to introduce these ideas during sessions at their annual conferences.

We thank the GATE Office, Los Angeles City Unified School District, LaRoyce Bell, and Lucy Hunt for supporting the first conference on Gifted Students of Diversity held at the University of Southern California.

# About the Authors

**Sandra N. Kaplan** has been a teacher and administrator of gifted programs in an urban school district in California. Currently, she is Clinical Professor in Teaching and Learning at the University of Southern California's Rossier School of Education. She has authored articles and books on the nature and scope of differentiated curriculum for gifted students. Her primary area of concern is modifying the core and differentiated curriculum to meet the needs of inner-city, gifted learners. Sandra is the past president of the California Association for the Gifted (CAG) and the National Association for Gifted Children (NAGC). Sandra has received the CAG Ruth A. Martinson Award and NAGC Distinguished Service Award in recognition of her contributions to gifted education.

**Irene Guzman** has been teaching in the Santa Ana Unified School District for fourteen years. She is currently teaching third grade at Heninger Elementary School. She has dedicated her efforts to differentiating the curriculum for gifted English language learners. She has worked closely with teachers to improve the specific needs for gifted students in the urban setting. Irene has worked under the USC Javits Grant as a mentor and a coach. She has also been a demonstration teacher and presenter at the California Association for the Gifted Conference and the USC summer institutes.

**Carol Ann Tomlinson** is the William Clay Parrish Jr. Professor of Educational Leadership, Foundations, and Policy at the University of Virginia's Curry School of Education and the department chair of Leadership, Foundations, and Policy. Prior to joining the University of Virginia's faculty, she was a classroom teacher for twenty-one years, working at the primary, middle, and high school levels. During that time, she also administered district programs for struggling and advanced learners and was recognized as Virginia's Teacher of the Year in 1974. Carol's present work focuses on curriculum and differentiated instruction. She was named outstanding professor at Curry in 2004 and won an all-university teaching award in 2008. Carol is the author of over 200 books, book chapters, articles, and professional development materials—many of them on differentiated instruction.

# Introduction

## *The Purposes of the Parallel Curriculum Model*

The Parallel Curriculum Model (PCM), like all other curriculum models, has been developed to meet a set of purposes. While these purposes share commonalities with other curriculum models, each curriculum model features specifics unique to it.

Curriculum models offer the educator a framework for professional decision making. They outline the intellectual territory educators can traverse for planning and implementing teaching and learning processes. Curricular models thus provide options that lead to goals.

PCM's framework defines learning experiences that reinforce each other and provide comprehensiveness of teaching and learning; the experiences thus complement each other in the attainment of a set of goals. PCM was also designed to meet many goals simultaneously. Each of the four parallel curriculum structures contributes to the attainment of a broad goal as well as the attainment of parallel-specific goals.

## MULTIPLE APPLICATIONS AND THE PARALLEL CURRICULUM MODEL

PCM was designed to be responsive to multiple populations and allows for different learning opportunities for diverse populations in varied contexts. The model originated as a way to challenge and provide academically rigorous curriculum experiences to gifted and high-ability learners. Although this set of learners provided the frame of reference for constructing the curriculum model, the opportunity then arose to consider the use of PCM for all types of learners. The multiple and versatile uses of PCM have been central to uncovering its specific applications to students of diversity in urban schools.

In his seminal work regarding curriculum construction, Tyler (1949) espoused the need for curriculum to be designed with three entities in mind: scholars, learners, and community. Based on this work, scholars include the body of educators and professionals who have outlined the important content and skills relevant to the current and future goals of a society. Learners embody the diversity of students within the classroom, school, or program. An analysis of this group revealed the multiple possibilities for implementing PCM for learners who manifested potential in particular subject areas but were not formally recognized as gifted or high achievers, and learners excited by the "opportunity to experience" academic challenges otherwise not available to them. Community involves the various contexts or settings related to schools, from those located in an urban center to those housed in rural areas, and the distinctive values, needs, and interests affecting schools within these areas.

## FLEXIBILITY OF THE PARALLEL CURRICULUM MODEL

PCM is intended to coexist with other curriculum theories and models and can augment the implementation of other curriculum. The notion of curriculums vying for the attention of teachers and programs is artificial. No one curriculum addresses all the needs of any particular program, group of educators, students, or community. The flexibility of a curriculum is one of its most important attributes. PCM has been developed to meet the flexibility of use demanded of high-quality curriculum.

## STRUCTURE OF THE PARALLEL CURRICULUM MODEL

PCM is comprised of four distinctive types of curricular experiences; each of these curricular experiences relates to the composition of the entire model, and all are intended to be used if the model is to be implemented with fidelity. That the entire four parallel curriculums must be used to be compliant with the intent of PCM, it should be noted, is not supported by all of the authors. While determining the characteristics of PCM important to students in an urban center, it became evident how each of the parallels contributed to their diverse needs. The non-negotiable use of all four parallel curriculums is responsive to urban learners. It introduces them to academically rigorous areas of curriculum often withheld from them because it is thought that they do not have the prerequisite content and skill and/or developmental or experiential readiness. In truth, this perception is a misconception that often blocks urban students from the very experiences that could enhance their exposure and mastery of basic as well as more sophisticated content and skills. The open-ended or divergent nature of many of the PCM curricular practices enables students to venture into the experience with varied prior knowledge and promotes an academic comfort not afforded in other types of curricular structures. The non-negotiable use of all four of the parallel curriculums meets the needs of academically diverse urban students by providing them with a set of curriculum venues that widens the range of opportunities and manifests latent potential that otherwise could remain undetected.

The Parallel Curriculum: A Model for Curriculum Planning

| The Core or Basic Curriculum | The Curriculum of Connections | The Curriculum of Practice | The Curriculum of Identity |
|---|---|---|---|
| The Core Curriculum is the foundational curriculum that establishes a rich framework of knowledge, understanding, and skills most relevant to the discipline. It is inclusive of and extends state and district expectations. It is the starting point or root system for all of the parallels in this model. The Core or Basic Curriculum: | This curriculum is derived from and extends the Core Curriculum. It is designed to help students encounter and interact with the key concepts, principles, and skills in a variety of settings, times, and circumstances. The Curriculum of Connections is designed to help students think about and apply key concepts, principles, and skills: | This curriculum is derived from and extends the Core Curriculum. Its purpose is to help students function with increasing skill and confidence in a discipline as professionals would function. It exists for the purpose of promoting students' expertise as practitioners of the discipline. The Curriculum of Practice asks students to: | This curriculum is derived from and extends the Core Curriculum. It is designed to help students see themselves in relation to the discipline both now and with possibilities for the future; understand the discipline more fully by connecting it with their lives and experiences; increase awareness of their preferences, strengths, interests, and need for growth; and think about themselves as stewards of the discipline who may contribute to it and/or through it. The Curriculum of Identity uses curriculum as a catalyst for self-definition and self-understanding, with the belief that by looking outward to the discipline, students can find a means of looking inward. The Curriculum of Identity asks students to: |
| • Is built on key facts, concepts, principles, and skills essential to a discipline<br>• Is coherent in its organization<br>• Is purposefully focused and organized to achieve essential outcomes<br>• Promotes understanding rather than rote learning<br>• Is taught in a meaningful context<br>• Causes students to grapple with ideas and questions, using both critical and creative thinking<br>• Is mentally and affectively engaging and satisfying to learners<br>• Results in evidence of worthwhile student production | • In a range of instances throughout the discipline<br>• Across disciplines<br>• Across time and time periods<br>• Across locations<br>• Across cultures<br>• Across times, locations, and cultures<br>• Through varied perspectives<br>• As impacted by various conditions (social, economic, technological political, etc.)<br>• Through the eyes of various people who affected and are affected by the ideas<br>• By examining links between concepts and development of the disciplines | • Understand the nature of the discipline in a real-world application manner<br>• Define and assume a role as a means of studying the discipline<br>• Understand the impact of this discipline on other disciplines and other disciplines on this discipline<br>• Become a disciplinary problem solver rather than being a problem solver using the subject matter of the discipline<br>• Understand and use the discipline as a means of looking at and making sense of the world<br>• Develop a means of escaping the rut of certainty about knowledge | • Reflect on their skills and interests as they relate to the discipline<br>• Understand ways in which their interests might be useful to the discipline and ways in which the discipline might serve as a means for helping them develop their skills and interests |

(Continued)

(Continued)

| The Core or Basic Curriculum | The Curriculum of Connections | The Curriculum of Practice | The Curriculum of Identity |
|---|---|---|---|
| | | • Comprehend the daily lives of workers or professionals in the discipline: working conditions, hierarchical structures, fiscal aspects of the work, peer or collegial dynamics<br>• Define and understand the implications of internal and external politics that impact the discipline<br>• Value and engage in the intellectual struggle of the discipline<br>• Function as a producer in the discipline<br>• Function as a scholar in the discipline | • Develop awareness of their modes of working as they relate to the modes of operation characteristic of the discipline<br>• Reflect on the impact of the discipline in the world, and self in the discipline<br>• Think about the impact of the discipline on the lives of others in the wider world<br>• Take intellectual samplings of the discipline for the purpose of experiencing self in relation to the discipline<br>• Examine the ethics and philosophy characteristic of the discipline and their implications<br>• Project themselves into the discipline<br>• Develop self in the context of the discipline and through interaction with the subject matter<br>• Develop a sense of both pride and humility related to both self and the discipline |

*Source:* C. A. Tomlinson et al., *The Parallel Curriculum: A Design to Develop Learner Potential and Challenge Advanced Learners*, 2nd edition. Thousand Oaks, CA: Corwin, 2009.

Parallel Curriculum Model: Relationship to Academic Diversity in Urban Schools

| Parallel Curriculum | Major Curriculum Emphasis | Relationship to Students in Urban Schools |
|---|---|---|
| Core Curriculum | Emphasizes the elements of content and skills of the basic curriculum at a more rigorous level. | The underperformance of students in inner city schools can be a consequence of lack of access to curriculum that has structural characteristics that challenge learning. |
| Curriculum of Connections | Emphasizes the associations within, between, and across disciplines, cultures, times, and places. | The ability to make connections allows students to build new learning (schemas) with existing learning as a means of making learning accessible, relevant, self-directed, and personalized. |
| Curriculum of Practice | Emphasizes the content and methodologies of the disciplines and the professionals or disciplinarians in various fields. | The appropriateness of curriculum that is culturally responsive addresses the contributions of groups to self and society. (Banks & McGee Banks, 2003) |
| Curriculum of Identity | Emphasizes developing one's own strength, preferences, and values. | The opportunities to learn about self and others and to understand how individuals manage multiple impressions of themselves is related to establishing self-identity. |

# RESPONDING TO STUDENT DIVERSITY WITH CURRICULUM DIVERSITY

The introduction of PCM to classrooms in urban schools brought into focus three factors that became the impetus for this text. First, the urban schools' classrooms reflected academic, cultural, economic, and linguistic diversity that often inhibited the selection and implementation of accelerated and/or enriched curriculums. Within a classroom setting, a population of twenty students can represent forty-four languages and a range of abilities, from students with a readiness to learn any subject beyond grade-level expectations to students learning formally for the first time in their educational careers. The range of experiences the students bring to the teaching and learning events is also varied by the boundaries of the neighborhood. Finally, students' experiences may be circumscribed by the encounters they have had as they migrated from one country to another before they settled. The cultural, linguistic, economic, and academic diversity of the students' needs requires diversity in the curriculum and pedagogy provided to them. The students' confrontation with curriculum and pedagogy that is not aligned with diverse learning needs representative of the class composition has resulted in the underachievement of students, in denial of the abilities of students, and in the misconceptions of teachers about the students' potential. Regardless of the students' perceived or verified level of academic performance, lack of curricular diversity can hamper academic success. PCM offers a collection of diverse learning experiences that reinforce basic content and skills, connect previously and newly acquired content to form new understanding, study the structure of the discipline, and relate learning to self as a scholar. Educators, parents, and teachers have recognized that it is essential to mediate the academic, cultural, economic, and linguistic differences among learners by matching their diversity to a diverse curriculum.

Second, the encounter with an academically rigorous curriculum such as PCM identified certain characteristics and learning needs of urban students. The emphasis on creating meaning rather than on restating what is already understood is integral to PCM. Students were being asked to establish links and associate ideas in the curriculum of connections, but learning experiences demanding provocative intellectual responses were outside the students' expected norms. Students initially blamed the curriculum, their teacher, and their peers for the intellectual struggles they were encountering. The absence of some of these skills and dispositions were not due to any one source; however, it is imperative to note that the needed skills had not always been appropriately activated in the school context because of the current curriculum's inability to help and/or demand that students access those skills (Moll & Greenberg, 1990). The initial resistance teachers observed to PCM by students appeared to be more often because of disinterest rather than an inability to participate actively. In his classic work, Tannenbaum (1983) refers to the nonintellectual factors that either release or inhibit a student's ability. Knowing the "rules of the game of cognition" is indispensable to success, according to Tannenbaum. He labeled the academic skill set as nonintellectual factors and included within it achievement motivation, self-concept, value preferences for learning, independence versus dependent orientation, personality structures, and stereotyping. The four parallels in the PCM curriculum provide the academic and social settings for the development of these nonintellectual factors.

Third, implementing PCM with students in heterogeneous classrooms catalyzed students who were not formerly identified as gifted to demonstrate abilities not visible in the traditional or regular curriculum. These expressions consequently resulted in new and different perspectives of these students by their teachers, peers, and parents. The identification of the abilities of students from diverse backgrounds is a spill-over benefit of PCM in a regular classroom. The opportunity to experience challenging curriculum that activated dormant abilities gave each student a new sense of self as a learner.

## URBAN CLASSROOM DYNAMICS

In an urban classroom, a third grader scans the room, trying to locate a peer he can emulate. He notices a peer waving his hand high in the air and answering the questions before he is even acknowledged by the teacher. "That's not me," he thinks. He scans the room again; all the other students are waiting docilely for the lesson to move forward. "That must be what you are supposed to do." He folds his hands, and as he remarks later to the teacher, "I swallowed the answer."

She really felt pleased about the story she wrote. She loved long sentences. They had more than seven words. She wondered if her seatmate would like her story, so she asked her if she wanted to read it. "Why should I read your story?" said her classmate. She was so startled by the comment that she simply said, "Oh well, it is not that good of a story."

"Come work with us. You can be the scribe for our group," said the girl as she waved to her friend. "What does the scribe do?" inquired the classmate. After the task was explained, her friend announced that he didn't want to be the scribe because he could not write or spell well. Everyone in the group laughed. "You get A's in math, so we know you can be a scribe," they said in unison. But he knew he could not be a good scribe. "Why wouldn't they listen to me?" he thought. He felt that they disliked him!

The teacher had introduced a controversial idea about whether or not to sell candy for the community mission. Students were raising their hands to give their opinions. "Yes, I think selling candy would be fun, and we could make lots of money." "No, I think candy is unhealthy." The students have different ideas. "What do you believe?" the teacher asked me. "I don't know," I said. But I was afraid to state my idea.

The teacher came up to me again. "Are you trying to do your best work?" she asked. I nodded my head. "Well, I can't understand how someone as smart as you is not doing better work. What's wrong?" she asked. I shook my head and shrugged my shoulders. "What did she mean?" I thought, because I was working as hard as I could.

- Fear of failure
- Hesitancy to participate
- Misunderstanding one's abilities, potential, and/or talent
- Inability to voice an opinion
- Erroneous expectations about success

These vignettes represent some of the behaviors indicative of students of diversity who are attempting to become familiar with a school's culture without losing their affiliations with and identity to other cultures to which they belong. Good and Brophy (2008) outline the salient characteristics of effective urban classrooms: high expectations and performance requirements, rigorous curriculum composed of significant content and skills, and instruction that stresses connections to prior knowledge and access to interactions among the community of learners.

These vignettes portray the classroom dynamics that thwart equity and access to academically rigorous curriculum by students of diversity. Scrutiny of the classroom dynamics reveals that all students do not comprehend how to attend and respond as learners in a community.

## DEVELOPING AN ACADEMIC SKILL SET

Learning how to identify themselves as learners and to participate in the classroom as a "scholar" is often expected of students but not necessarily a part of traditionally taught, school-based skills. It is erroneous to assume that perceiving oneself as a student and performing actively in various teaching and learning events are natural consequences of attending school. It is also erroneous to believe that the caregiver unit is responsible for teaching this academic skill set. The consequences of not having a well-developed sense of self as a learner are severe and have led to articulating these skills and deliberately integrating them into a well-defined curricular structure. PCM provides the opportunity to teach these skills and dispositions through the different contexts of its parallel structures, thus affording students opportunities to implement these skills while achieving varied outcomes.

The academic skill set for PCM has been divided into sections. Each section is defined by a set of subskills related to specific objectives that allow students to (1) become aware of the nature and dimensions of each of the skills, (2) value them as part of the students' repertoire, and (3) acquire the responsibility to activate these skills appropriately. These academic skills, which relate to learning how to become a student, need to be consistently reintroduced and reinforced. While students do improve in implementing these skills, they need continual practice to become "life-long learners."

The following skills are included in the academic skill set:

- Scholarly Dispositions
- Participation Skills
- Self-Advocacy Skills
- Presentation Skills

**Scholarly Dispositions** identify the attitude scholars need to be productive learners. The potential of a learner is contingent on recognizing how to initiate and monitor behaviors that underscore the concept of self as a student, creator, researcher, and worker. Scholarly Dispositions specify the goals students must accept and respect for realizing their attributes as successful learners.

The following specific subskills are included within Scholarly Dispositions:

- Developing an Interest
- Developing Tenacity
- Confronting Failure
- Recognizing Intellectual Strengths

**Participation Skills** represent the category of academic skills related to teaching students how to become engaged and maintain involvement in the teaching and learning process. The seeming disinterest students portray to teachers and peers may not be what appearances indicate. In some situations, students do not know how to initiate their engagement in classroom activity because of various cultural values, exposure to different educational systems prior to entering their current school, and insufficient language development to decode the entry points for participation. It is interesting to note that the same type of perplexity that consumes adult learners and stops them from becoming participants also affects younger learners; this fact should help educators become more aware of the skills required in learning how to participate.

The following specific subskills are included within Participation Skills:

- Questioning
- Asking for Clarification

- Restating
- Acknowledging Peers

**Self-Advocacy Skills** include subskills for gaining techniques needed for students to become visible, active, and forceful individuals in a lesson or the classroom. Among students in an urban school setting, the ability to define oneself as a learner is obscured by several factors: (1) pacing charts that require certain standards or information and skills to be taught within a particular time frame; (2) the demand to meet grade-level proficiency, which becomes more dominant than the request to practice behaviors that are not measured on a test but, rather, in the process of learning; and (3) the philosophical belief held by some educators and parents that neither the school nor society are concerned about developing one's presence as a scholar. Acquiring a presence as a student is the end goal of Self-Advocacy Skills.

The following specific subskills are included within Self-Advocacy Skills:

- Establishing a Voice
- Building Confidence
- Establishing an Identity
- Multiple Group Membership

**Presentation Skills** comprise a fourth category of the academic skills set and are aimed at promoting students' abilities to participate effectively with their peers and to overcome elements that manifest themselves as insecurities that inhibit sharing and discussion. The Presentation Skills are presented as charts and worksheets for teachers to use.

- Talking Steps
- Ways to Say It
- Engaging the Audience
- Staying on Target

## INTRODUCTION TO THE PCM FOCUS LESSONS

The PCM Focus Lessons adhere to specific learning theories.

- Dependency on the social interactions inherent in sociocultural learning.
  - o Basically, the learning that takes place among a group of students is a form of enculturation as members share the knowledge and skills of the classroom culture. A goal of these lessons is to establish the classroom culture as one wherein students assume the role of scholars. The concept of situated learning—learning applied in a particular setting to attain specific purposes—is vital to students of academic diversity. The lesson plans help establish a classroom culture wherein the students can align themselves with the values and behaviors of this culture.

- Relevancy to a constructivist approach to teaching and learning that emphasizes the student's ability to construct meaning as a result of the teaching/learning experiences.
  - o The expectations are that students will be active participants, working collaboratively with peers to seek understanding, and that they will use the resources and tools teachers provide to mediate or scaffold their learning.

- Emphasis on shifting responsibility for learning from the teacher to the student.
  - ○ Although the teacher follows the learning experiences and provides the described structured assistance needed for student performance, strategies such as asking questions, stimulating discussions, modeling, and rendering cues for self-motivation help students share responsibilities for learning.
- Stress on the concept of challenge in learning experiences, which stimulates curiosity and outlines the path to deeper and broader content and skill areas for students to explore.
  - ○ Teachers need to arouse students to recognize and appreciate the goals and values of "difficult" learning experiences, defined as a way to further rather than annihilate their abilities.

## LESSON PLAN FORMAT

A specific lesson plan format was selected to present the curriculum and guide instruction for many reasons. The lesson plan design outlines the stages and sequence by which students can assimilate the content and practice the skills fundamental to the objective of the lesson. The organized presentation of activities within the context of a lesson reduces opportunities for what the literature on curriculums labels "disjointed incremental learning" or the presentation of isolated activities. The lesson plan format provides continuity and comprehensiveness to a set of learning experiences directed at attaining a specific outcome or objective. Each lesson plan could be considered a mini unit of study and is not intended to be implemented within a single day or allocated to a particular time frame. It is anticipated that each lesson plan will take more than one day to teach and will necessitate scheduling multiple encounters over a designated period of time. The determination of time for each lesson should also be responsive to factors such as the juxtaposition of the lesson plan's objective to the standards-based curriculum. The developmental appropriateness of the objectives to the age and/or grade level, any readiness needs that must be provided to students to achieve lesson outcomes, and teacher preparation to affect appropriate implementation with the greatest fidelity to the lesson plan are factors ultimately determining the amount of time to be allocated to a lesson.

The lesson plans in this book are arranged in the following format:

### PCM Focus

The focus statement identifies the specific content and/or skill(s) to be taught. An area of focus defines the content or subject matter and applies it within the context or environments and situations in which its purposes and effects are explained and practiced. The skill is presented as a behavior to be operationalized by the students and to be incorporated as part of the students' repertoire as they assume responsibility for themselves and their learning.

### Objective

The objective or intended outcome describes the underlying cognitive and affective goal that relates to and underscores the PCM Focus.

## Motivate

This section evokes students' interest in a learning experience that has meaning and value to them. The lessons are not aimed at being "fun," nor do they use extrinsic reward features often included to arouse and sustain student involvement. The motivation section of the lesson is based on self-determination and interest theory reported by Good and Brophy (2008). Self-determination theory stresses the importance of the social environment as a means to help students gain autonomy in exercising skills and assimilating content. Interest theory reinforces the importance of activities that emphasize intriguing experiences. All PCM Focus content areas and skills stress the development of student autonomy to learn the content and skills and foster experiences that strive to arouse the student's worth and enjoyment in learning.

## Activate Prior Knowledge

This section of the lesson plan enables students to connect new to existing content and skills and thus forge new learning. Basically, students are acknowledged for the competencies and understandings they bring into the learning experience. The activation of prior knowledge is mediated by instructional strategies addressing creative and critical thinking in the problem-solving process. The divergent nature of the learning experiences allows students to exercise options that encourage them to define themselves as students.

## Relationship to PCM

Every PCM Focus relates to each of the four parallel curriculums. This application process has several purposes:

- To note the effectiveness of the content and/or skill in the varied curriculums defined by the Core, Practice, Connections, and Identity sections
- To recognize how the variations in curricular applications introduce nuances in the use and meaning of the content and skills
- To reinforce the realization that open-ended or divergent thinking creates responses that add rather than diminish a student's contribution to self and the group

# IMPLEMENTING THE LESSON PLAN

The importance of the lesson plans lay in what they are designed to achieve and not in the means by which they are implemented. The lessons can be taught to a class in whole-group or small-group settings using these criteria to make curricular decisions:

1. Determine if the lesson will be taught as a corollary to the standards-based or regular curriculum.

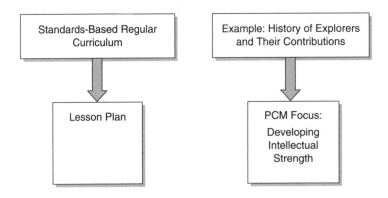

Central to this decision is to establish where the lesson plan will appropriately intersect the regular curriculum. The most effective intersection will readily accommodate the PCM Focus without distorting either the regular or lesson plan curricular objectives.

2. Determine if the lesson plan should be the means to initiate the standards-based curriculum.

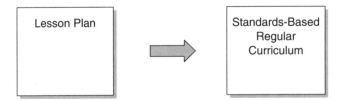

With this decision, the lesson plan prefaces any experiences that follow and establishes the rationale for connecting other learnings to ensure curriculum continuity and comprehensibility. Basically, the Core Curriculum Parallel is the easiest or most expedient entry point for connecting the regular curriculum and the PCM Focus lesson plan.

3. Decide if the lesson plan should be a follow-up or an extension to the standards-based curriculum. When placing the lesson plan as a follow-up or extension, one concern is to ensure it is not relegated to the position of an addendum rather than as an integral feature of the curriculum.

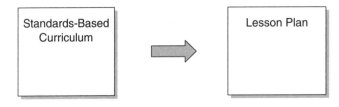

# LESSON PLAN SCHEDULING

The decision to teach a single lesson plan over a specific period of time or to teach the lesson in segments over time is dependent on several factors. Regardless of the decision on how to proceed, the lessons demand preparation from the teacher and receptivity to the PCM Focus from the students. Preparation by the teacher should include the following:

- Reviewing the lesson's purpose and how the sections reinforce the attainment of the lesson's objective.
- Gathering and organizing the materials, such as pictures and charts, so they are readily available for the lesson. It should be noted that stopping the lesson in process to gather or construct needed materials detracts from its impact on the students.
- Selecting a natural break in the lesson where ending that section will not inhibit learning the concept or skill or give the students premature closure concerning the attainment of the lesson's objective. The following are some statements used by a teacher to clearly indicate that the lesson is ended but not completed:
  - o Let's summarize in our own words what we have learned thus far.
  - o Let's identify what we need to remember for using this skill later in this lesson.
  - o Let's list the questions the lesson has stimulated us to ask so we can answer them when we continue with this lesson.
  - o Let's store in our "Intellectual Bank" the information we have found to be most important thus far in the lesson.

The lesson plans have been developed to introduce and reinforce particular areas identified under the academic skill sets. The collection of lessons for each academic skill (Scholarly Dispositions, Participation Skills, Self-Advocacy Skills, and Presentation Skills) can be used in two distinctly different ways:

1. The lessons can be used independently as determined by student and/or teacher assessment of need and appropriate alignment to the standards-based or regular curriculum.

2. The lessons can be used as a unit of study to reinforce specific academic skills and can be implemented in sequence over time.

While there is no one way to implement the lessons, using the lessons as a unit of study does allow for the continuity and comprehensiveness that units of study afford the learner. In other words, the collection of five lessons that all relate to Participation Skills forms a unit of study that can be taught over a predetermined period of time. Implementing the lessons as single entities requires that the teacher make sure that the lessons have a relevant connection to the standard, topic, or unit of study defined in the regular or basic curriculum.

The lessons have been designed to teach across grade levels with no specific relationship to any one grade or age level. Adjustments in pacing, vocabulary, resources, and amount of teacher and peer assistance make them age/grade-level specific.

## DEPTH AND COMPLEXITY

General discussions about responding to the needs of gifted and highly able students often address providing depth and complexity of learning. There are many definitions of depth and complexity. For some educators, depth and complexity refer to the difficulty of achieving the content and skills. Other educators equate depth and complexity with the quantity of elements within an assignment, which is usually reflected in the student's results. The ambiguity of the terms *depth* and *complexity* was the impetus to define the concepts by a group of educators convened by the California Department of Education and funded in part from a Jacob Javits Gifted and Talented Program, U.S. Department of Education (1994). The high expectations reflected by Advanced Placement free-response questions, conventional wisdom about what teachers and parents target as successful scholarship for gifted and high-ability students, and the academic competencies required for college were used to determine the scope of depth and complexity.

The use of prompts to stimulate understanding or serve as catalysts for inquiry has been addressed in several theories of learning. The definition of depth and complexity applied in this book references both a publication by the California Department of Education (1994) and the work from a Jacob Javits Department of Education grant awarded to the University of Southern California (Project T.W.O., 1997). Depth and complexity are indicated by both narrative and iconic representations throughout the lesson plans (see the following table). These prompts are also incorporated within the California Department of Education GATE standards (2001, 2005) and are used to define the elements that make up the principles of differentiation for gifted and high-ability students.

Facilitating the Understanding of Depth and Complexity

**Note to the teacher:** This chart identifies key questions, thinking skills, and dimensions of *depth* and *complexity*.

- *Key questions* can be used in the context of lesson plans to probe understanding and to prompt students during discussions.
- *Thinking skills* can be used to initiate the type of cognitive operation or thinking that will best prompt each of the dimensions of depth and complexity.
- The *resources* listed are the most logical references in which to locate the type of information required by each of the dimensions of depth and complexity. Teachers may add to any of these lists as appropriate.

| Icons | Prompt | Key Questions | Thinking Skills | Resources |
|---|---|---|---|---|
| | Language of the disciplines | What terms or words are specific to the work of the _____ ? (discipline)<br><br>What tools does the _____ (discipline) use? | • Categorize<br>• Identify | • Texts<br>• Biographies |
| | Details | What are its attributes?<br><br>What features characterize this?<br><br>What specific elements define this?<br><br>What distinguishes this from other things? | • Identify traits<br>• Describe<br>• Differentiate<br>• Compare/contrast<br>• Prove with evidence<br>• Observe | • Pictures<br>• Diaries or journals<br>• Poetry |
| | Patterns | What are the reoccurring events?<br><br>What elements, events, and ideas are repeated over time?<br><br>What was the order of events?<br><br>How can we predict what will come next? | • Determine relevant versus irrelevant<br>• Summarize<br>• Make analogies<br>• Discriminate between same and different<br>• Relate | • Time lines<br>• Other chronological lists |

(Continued)

(Continued)

| Icons | Prompt | Key Questions | Thinking Skills | Resources |
|---|---|---|---|---|
| | Trends | What ongoing factors have influenced this study?<br><br>What factors have contributed to this study? | • Prioritize<br>• Determine cause and effect<br>• Predict<br>• Relate<br>• Formulate questions<br>• Hypothesize | • Journals<br>• Newspapers<br>• Graphs<br>• Charts |
| | Unanswered questions | What is still not understood about this area, topic, study, or discipline?<br><br>What is yet unknown about this area, topic, study, or discipline?<br><br>In what ways is the information incomplete or lacking in explanation? | • Recognize fallacies<br>• Note ambiguity<br>• Distinguish fact versus fiction and opinion<br>• Formulate questions<br>• Problem solve<br>• Identify missing information<br>• Test assumptions | • Multiple and varied resources<br>• Comparative analyses of autobiographical and current nonfiction articles, etc. |
| | Rules | How is this structured?<br><br>What are the stated and unstated causes related to the description or explanation of what we are studying? | • Generalize<br>• Hypothesize<br>• Judge credibility | • Editorials<br>• Essays<br>• Laws<br>• Theories |
| | Ethics | What dilemmas or controversies are involved in this area, topic, study, or discipline?<br><br>What elements can be identified that reflect bias, prejudice, and discrimination? | • Judge with criteria<br>• Determine bias | • Editorials<br>• Essays<br>• Autobiographies<br>• Journals |
| | Big ideas, generalizations, principles, and theories | What overarching statement best describes what is being studied?<br><br>What general statement includes what is being studied? | • Prove with evidence<br>• Generalize<br>• Identify the main idea | • Quotations<br>• Discipline-related essays |

| Icons | Prompt | Key Questions | Thinking Skills | Resources |
|---|---|---|---|---|
| FUTURE PRESENT PAST (circular icon) | Over time | How are ideas related among the past, present, and future?<br><br>How are these ideas related within or during a particular time period?<br><br>How has time affected the information?<br><br>How and why do things change or remain the same? | • Relate<br>• Sequence<br>• Order | • Time lines<br>• Text<br>• Biographies<br>• Autobiographies<br>• Historical documents |
| (glasses icon) | Different points of view | What are the opposing viewpoints?<br><br>How do different people and characters see this event or situation? | • Argue<br>• Determine bias<br>• Classify | • Biographies<br>• Autobiographies<br>• Mythologies and legends versus nonfiction accounts<br>• Debates |

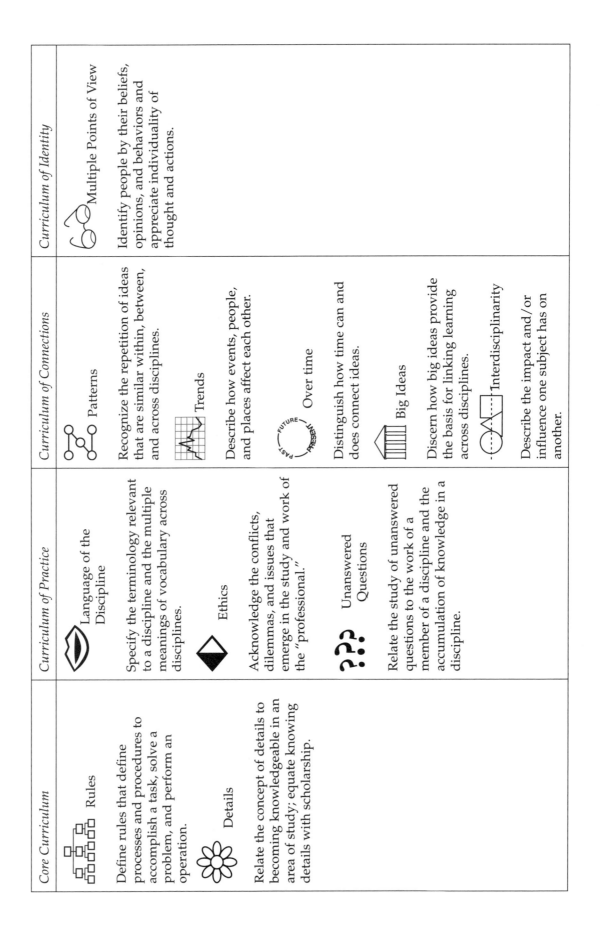

| Core Curriculum | Curriculum of Practice | Curriculum of Connections | Curriculum of Identity |
| --- | --- | --- | --- |
| **Rules** | **Language of the Discipline** | **Patterns** | **Multiple Points of View** |
| Define rules that define processes and procedures to accomplish a task, solve a problem, and perform an operation. | Specify the terminology relevant to a discipline and the multiple meanings of vocabulary across disciplines. | Recognize the repetition of ideas that are similar within, between, and across disciplines. | Identify people by their beliefs, opinions, and behaviors and appreciate individuality of thought and actions. |
| **Details** | **Ethics** | **Trends** | |
| Relate the concept of details to becoming knowledgeable in an area of study; equate knowing details with scholarship. | Acknowledge the conflicts, dilemmas, and issues that emerge in the study and work of the "professional." | Describe how events, people, and places affect each other. | |
| | **Unanswered Questions** | **Over time** | |
| | Relate the study of unanswered questions to the work of a member of a discipline and the accumulation of knowledge in a discipline. | Distinguish how time can and does connect ideas. | |
| | | **Big Ideas** | |
| | | Discern how big ideas provide the basis for linking learning across disciplines. | |
| | | **Interdisciplinarity** | |
| | | Describe the impact and/or influence one subject has on another. | |

18

# 1

# **Scholarly Dispositions**

## LESSON A: DEVELOPING AN INTEREST (I)

**PCM Focus:** Developing an interest

**Objective:** Students will develop an understanding of how interest can be developed and nurtured by the individual's actions.

## MOTIVATE

Present the 🏛 big idea and the following pictures to the students:

### Being interested is a natural phenomenon or activity.

Refer to the pictures to hypothesize and test the meaning of the 🏛 big idea or theoretical statement. For example, students could respond that the interests of the Curious Bear are food, the feel of the metal on the trash can, and so on.

Generate a list of possible interests depicted by each picture:

| Curious Bear | Scientific Curiosity | Studious Boy |
|---|---|---|
|  |  |  |

## ACTIVATE PRIOR KNOWLEDGE

Discuss the meaning of an "inventory" and the multiple reasons and places for taking or making an inventory: at retail stores to determine merchandise stock, in the classroom to ascertain available supplies, etc.

Have students take an inventory of the inside of their desks.

Introduce the following form for students to conduct their own interest inventory. Provide opportunities for students to share their inventories.

Compare the Interest Inventory to other types of inventories.

Ask students to prioritize interests in each category with regard to ✿ details such as time, resources, and effort. Discuss how and why interests change ◯ over time.

| Interest Inventory | | |
|---|---|---|
| At Home | At School | At Play |
| 1.<br>2.<br>3.<br>4. | 1.<br>2.<br>3.<br>4. | 1.<br>2.<br>3.<br>4. |
| Prioritize<br>1.<br>2.<br>3.<br>4. | Prioritize<br>1.<br>2.<br>3.<br>4. | Prioritize<br>1.<br>2.<br>3.<br>4. |

## RELATIONSHIP TO PCM

### Core Curriculum

Literature—Identify behaviors of fiction or nonfiction characters that exemplify "interest."

Create a chart for articulating the various interests of the characters found in different genres. Note the example of a completed entry on the chart.

## Literary Characters' Interests

| Genre | Characters | Interest | Effects of Interest |
|---|---|---|---|
| Fairy tale | Goldilocks | Exploring food to eat | Deciding which food was "just right" for her to eat |
|  |  |  |  |

Use the completed chart to identify ⚬⚬ patterns depicting the interests of characters in different genres.

## Curriculum of Practice

Discuss the steps in the process of problem solving:

- Define the problem
- Gather information
- Organize information
- Select a solution

Acknowledge the value of problem solving in a chosen discipline. Research the role of interest for a disciplinarian to problem solve in that discipline.

Use the graph-type chart to record and display the degree to which the chosen disciplinarian in the selected discipline invests interest in each step of problem solving. Instruct students to color in the degree each step is used by the disciplinarian to problem solve.

| Disciplinarians | | | |
|---|---|---|---|
| **Steps** | **Disciplinarian** <br> **Degree of Interest** - - - - - - - - - - - - - - - - → | | |
| Define the problem |  |  |  |
| Gather information |  |  |  |
| Organize information |  |  |  |
| Select a solution |  |  |  |

## Curriculum of Connections

Reintroduce the 🏛 big idea and have students apply it to each of the areas they are studying to find evidence that support it.

> # Being interested is a natural phenomenon or activity.

Complete a chart as a class to support the 🏛 big idea using examples from the topics currently under study in the curriculum. (Note the example on the chart.)

| Building Evidence to Support the 🏛 Big Idea | | | |
|---|---|---|---|
| | ↑ | ↑ | ↑ | ↑ |
| Example | Reading mythology | | |
| Example | Using a telescope | | |
| Topic | Astronomy | Topic | Topic |

## Curriculum of Identity

Ask students to discuss ways in which they build an interest, using the diagram as a means to prompt discussion.

| Identify parts that make a whole | Asking about its use | Getting more information | Thinking about its value to you and others |
|---|---|---|---|

**The interest I developed:**

Instruct students to maintain a journal describing their commitment to "develop a *new* interest." Discuss the implications of the interest short and long term (◯ over time) and for different contexts: schooling, recreation, leisure.

## LESSON B: DEVELOPING AN INTEREST (II)

**PCM Focus**: Developing an interest

**Objective:** Students will be able to comprehend the value of developing and sustaining an interest.

## MOTIVATE

Display the following set of pictures and ask students to formulate questions about what messages the pictures are communicating about people and their interests. Discuss when and why the students display similar behaviors of "being interested in something."

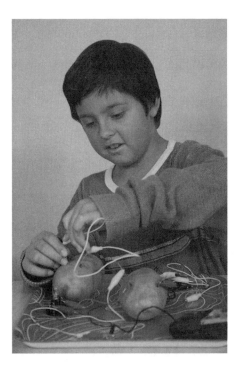

Discuss the "what ifs" or the consequences of the episodes presented in the following scenes that illustrate devotion to an interest:

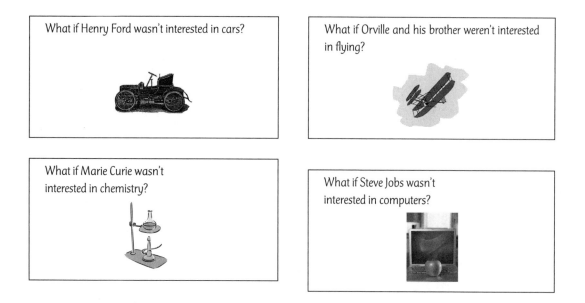

What if Henry Ford wasn't interested in cars?

What if Orville and his brother weren't interested in flying?

What if Marie Curie wasn't interested in chemistry?

What if Steve Jobs wasn't interested in computers?

Introduce the collection of words that define "interest"—value, attentiveness, concern, enthusiasm, and curiosity.

Discuss the implications of these terms to the actions and behaviors of people who have been successful by completing the following retrieval chart.

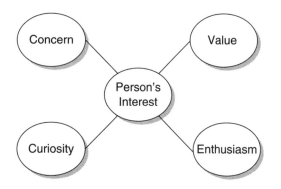

Research additional information about an individual to describe the attributes that drove the person's interest.

## ACTIVATE PRIOR KNOWLEDGE

Present the following Interest Indicator:

| Interest Indicator | | | | |
|---|---|---|---|---|
| 1 | 2 | 3 | 4 | 5 |
| Becoming aware of something | Valuing something | Recognizing how something "matches" you | Understanding how you benefit from something | Developing an interest: immersing oneself in something |

Apply the Interest Indicator to a previously read biography or autobiography.

Discuss how the indicator could be a ⚇ pattern in developing an interest.

Identify how ⩕ trends influence interests.

Have each student apply the procedural steps of the Interest Indicator to one of their own interests.

## RELATIONSHIP TO PCM

### Core Curriculum

Research the means by which authors *stimulate interest* in a character, setting, and/ or problem in a story by using words, actions, and interactions.

### Curriculum of Practice

Read a biography on an inventor, scientist, author, or historical figure.

Research how the selected individual became interested in their field of study. Use the Interest Indicator to chart the individual's experiences to develop an interest.

| Interest Indicator | | | | |
|---|---|---|---|---|
| 1 | 2 | 3 | 4 | 5 |
| Becoming aware of something | Valuing something | Recognizing how something "matches" you | Understanding how you benefit from something | Developing an interest: immersing oneself in something |

## Curriculum of Connections

Research how advertisements create an interest in different areas and then debate this statement: *The art of persuasion can stimulate interest.*

## Curriculum of Identity

Discuss the concept that people are a composition of their interests: *How do our choices at school and at play reflect our interests?*

Instruct each student to create a collage or mosaic that is a personal reflection of the interests they have.

## LESSON C: DEVELOPING TENACITY

**PCM Focus:** Developing tenacity

**Objective:** Students will be able to relate the importance of tenacity or task commitment to learning and academic success.

## MOTIVATE

Use these endeavors of famous people as the backdrop for a discussion about a sense of industry or tenacity.

It took Michelangelo four years to paint the Sistine Chapel.

It took Marco Polo three years to travel the Silk Road.

It took twenty-one years to complete the Statue of Liberty, from an idea to a statue.

Discuss the relationship between time spent on a task and the value or appreciation attributed to the task.

Respond to the concept of tenacity in a question: How do we determine if the time spent on a task is worth the investment?

Relate the concept of tenacity to patterns of behaviors. Discuss the effects of tenacity over time and the ethics involved in using one's tenacity.

Note examples of the ethical issues in using one's tenacity:

- An individual who is so preoccupied with work that he/she does not have time to be with friends or to complete assigned chores.
- An individual who commits all his/her time to one subject but not to others.

## ACTIVATE PRIOR KNOWLEDGE

- Provide students with this set of 3 × 5 cards:

| Contribution | Effort | Extrinsic Reward | |
|---|---|---|---|
| Time | Drive | Intrinsic Reward | Fame |

- Inform students that each of these cards represents vocabulary or terminology related to how and why people are tenacious or stick to the task (task commitment).
- Refer to the following set of school-based experiences and ask students to identify which of the terms has most significantly affected their practice of tenacity during each of the tasks. For example, a student could respond that the tenacity exerted while "studying for a spelling test" is related to "Extrinsic Reward."

## A Day at School

- **Studying for a spelling test**

- **Practicing addition and subtraction**

- **Examining cells under a microscope**

- **Researching in a book**

- **Writing a story**

# RELATIONSHIP TO PCM

## Core Curriculum

Select a topic to introduce the students to the concept of writing an independent report.

Use the following chart for the students to continually record the degree of tenacity they have expended on each segment of their independent report.

### Tracking Tenacity

Name:_____

| Steps in the Report Project | Degree of Tenacity | | | Reason for Tenacity |
|---|---|---|---|---|
| | None | Some | A Lot | |
| Selecting a topic | | | | |
| Developing questions | | | | |
| Researching the questions | | | | |
| Writing the report, with information that answers the questions | | | | |

Use the students' Tracking Tenacity charts to synthesize how and why students use tenacity.

## Curriculum of Practice

Discuss the statement that "tenacity is a necessary characteristic of many professions."

Identify the degree to which tenacity is a required attribute in discipline-related professions and the ways tenacity is practiced by disciplinarians such as the following:

- Botanists
- Economists
- Geologists
- Historians

Introduce behaviors that reflect tenacity exhibited by disciplinarians:

- Tolerating ambiguity
- Waiting or exhibiting patience
- Working to resolve the unknown
- Digging for ❀ details

## Curriculum of Connections

Present this set of words on a chart framed by the word *tenacity*.

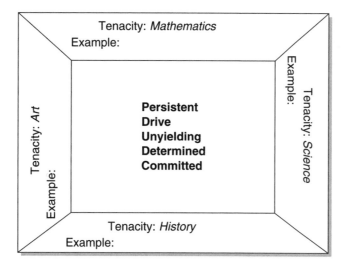

Explain that the words in the center of the frame are synonyms for tenacity.

Find examples across the disciplines to illustrate the role tenacity plays in each discipline to complete the frame.

Instruct students to categorize the behavior descriptive of tenacity while performing various school-related activities. Compare the entries on this chart to the completed frame.

| Activity | Problem Solving | Writing a Story | Playing a Game |
|---|---|---|---|
| | Behavior: | Behavior: | Behavior: |

## Curriculum of Identity

Discuss why and how tenacity is related to these proverbs:

- "Energy and persistence conquer all things."
- "Without sweat and toil no work is made perfect."
- "Keep your nose to the grindstone."

Create a *tenacity chain*.

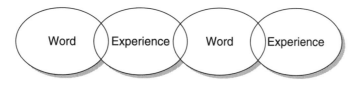

Instruct students to use the words that define tenacity in one circle and match the word with an experience that exemplifies the students' expression of tenacity in the second circle. Note that chains can be constructed to include experiences across various content areas or disciplines.

Discuss what has been learned about tenacity *and* its relationship to experiences in the disciplines from creating the tenacity chain.

## LESSON D: DETERMINING RELEVANCE

**PCM Focus:** Determining relevance

**Objective:** Students will be able to define and describe the importance of the content and skills they have learned by determining the relevance of their learning experiences.

## MOTIVATE

Refer to the following statements to stimulate a discussion focused on the concept of "relevance":

**WHY?**

Why should I learn today about what happened in 1476?

Why should I learn to +, - , ×, ÷ if I have a calculator?

Why should I learn how to read when I can get books on tape?

## ACTIVATE PRIOR KNOWLEDGE

Have students make a list of all the things they have learned in a day/week at school. Instruct them to prioritize or order the "lessons learned" with respect to the categories on this chart:

| Lessons Learned | | | |
|---|---|---|---|
| **What I learned:** 1 | | **Prioritizing what I learned by** *interest:* 2 | |
| **Prioritizing what I learned by** *difficulty:* 3 | | **Prioritizing what I learned by** *importance:* 4 | |

Define the patterns of learning reflected by the priorities students have recorded.

Discuss how and why priorities change according to different situations such as interest, difficulty of task, and time allocated to the task.

Relate the concept of *priority* to the concept of *relevance.* Answer the question: *What determines if something you learn is relevant?*

## RELATIONSHIP TO PCM

## Core Curriculum

Define the relevance or importance of a subject learned to different variables: age, goals, work that is required or assigned, other areas taught within the school day, and so on.

## Curriculum of Practice

Discuss how the same body of knowledge has different values for different disciplines by coloring in the selected value on the chart.

| Relevance | | | | |
|---|---|---|---|---|
| What was learned: _____ | | | | |
| Its value to the disciplines: | | | | |
| Level of Relevance | Science | Social Studies | Math | Language Arts |
| High | | | | |
| Medium | | | | |
| Low | | | | |

Use the completed chart to define the variability of the relevance of the same learned content or skill as it is used within the disciplines; identify the factors that cause this variability.

## Curriculum of Connections

Find evidence to prove, validate, and/or support this 🏛 big idea:

> # The value of something is relative.

Encourage students to select at least two areas or topics in different disciplines to validate the 🏛 big idea. Demonstrate to the students how the value of a skill, such as "prove with evidence," changes in different contexts. *Example:* "Prove with evidence" has a significant value in the study of density and a less significant value in creating or writing a story because . . .

## Curriculum of Identity

Research the life of an author and inventor to support the concept that *information* has different values or relevance to different people depending on *why* and *how* the information is used.

# LESSON E: CONFRONTING FAILURE

**PCM Focus:** Confronting failure

**Objective:** Students will develop an understanding of the positive effects of failure as a scholar and student.

## MOTIVATE

Discuss how learning can take place in a variety of situations and conditions using these questions as prompts:

- How can you learn about plants from a garden just as you can learn about plants from a book in a classroom?
- How can you learn math while you are at a baseball game just as you can learn math from a problem on the whiteboard?
- How can you learn from someone who knows more or less than you?
- How can you learn from a mistake or error?

Identify the ❁ details and ⚛ patterns reflecting the responses to the previous questions.

Discuss the positive characteristics or traits of failure. Ask students to define what can be learned from examining each of the following situations depicting "failure."

Present the 🏛 big idea as a statement:

## Failure is a teacher.

Direct students to verify this statement using episodes from their own lives.

## ACTIVATE PRIOR KNOWLEDGE

Introduce and discuss the following "Learning from Failure" patterns:

| A | Learning ──────────→                                    Failure |
|---|---|
|   | Learning until you meet failure and then stopping. |

| B | Learning ──────────→ Failure          Learning in a new way - - - - - - →|
|---|---|
|   | Learning and meeting failure and then continue learning in a new way. |

| C | Learning ──────────→ Failure          Learning in a new way - - - - - →|
|---|---|
|   | ←────── Going back |
|   | Learning, meeting failure, going back to try again, and then learning in a new way. |

Discuss the common characteristics found in each "Learning from Failure" pattern: risk-taking, repetition, embarrassment, drive, rewards, tenacity, and self-concept.

Provide students with an opportunity to discuss "the times when" one or more of the "Learning From Failure" patterns was a *real* event in the students' lives.

Relate the concept that recognizing a pattern of behavior affects one's perceptions of self over time.

Facilitate a discussion with students so they can articulate when they are more "prone or susceptible" to failure in one subject versus another.

# RELATIONSHIP TO PCM

## Core Curriculum

Present the following set of fictitious work samples and use them to facilitate discussion related to these questions:

1. What is the error?
2. How can errors become a learning experience?

**An Illustration of a Kangaroo**

The teacher wrote: This is a well-developed kangaroo. Please redo the tail of the animal. It is not correct.

**Math Problem**

✓

1. $(3 + 3) + 2 = 8$
   $6 + 2 = 3$

2. $(4 + 5) = 6 + 3$
   $(2 + 2) + 1 + 5 = 10$

The teacher wrote: How can you check your answers? Review operational signs.

**The Ocean**

The ocean is like the wind.
It moves fast and high.

The teacher wrote: Is this analogy really clear? Please rewrite.

Consider continuing the learning experience with anonymous examples of student work.

## Curriculum of Practice

Play the YouTube "Famous Failures" to initiate a discussion about how individuals in their fields met failure and still attained success.

Introduce the 🏛 big idea:

## Failure provides a new perspective.

Research a prominent individual to identify information that supports the idea that failure can be perceived from 👓 multiple perspectives:

1. Failure as "closing the door" versus "opening the door" to opportunity.

2. Failure as a negative or positive influence in assuming a role or taking action.

3. Failure as the signature of a "winner" approaching something new.

Consider continuing the learning experience with anonymous examples of student work.

## Curriculum of Connections

Instruct students to collect evidence across the disciplines to prove that *failure* is a universal experience.

Have students conduct investigations to show how failure led to progress in various ancient and contemporary cultures.

## Curriculum of Identity

Reinforce the concept that we "learn from failure" and that "failure defines how we approach what we learn." Use this scenario for promoting the discussion:

Imagine you are going to learn something new. How do previous failures shape your thinking and actions while learning this new "thing"?

Complete the chart to synthesize understanding of how failure influences our approaches to new learning.

| Failure situation | What I learned from the failure | How the failure helps me learn something new |
|---|---|---|
| | | |
| | | |
| | | |

## LESSON F: INTELLECTUAL STRENGTHS

**PCM Focus:** Intellectual strengths

**Objective:** Students will be able to relate the concept of "intellectual strength" to the specific attributes or traits that define potential, ability, and/or "giftedness" of the scholar or achiever.

## MOTIVATE

Present students with an array of pictures that show strength:

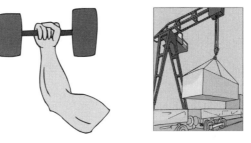

Discuss the feature each of these pictures has in common.

Introduce the relationship between physical and academic strengths and discuss the ⬤ language of the discipline: intellectual strength.

Prompt students to identify the intellectual strengths represented by the following people after reading their short biographies.

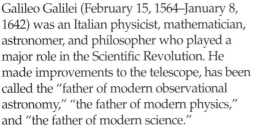

Galileo Galilei (February 15, 1564–January 8, 1642) was an Italian physicist, mathematician, astronomer, and philosopher who played a major role in the Scientific Revolution. He made improvements to the telescope, has been called the "father of modern observational astronomy," "the father of modern physics," and "the father of modern science."

John Herschel Glenn Jr. (July 18, 1921– ) is a former astronaut who became the first American to orbit the Earth. He flew aboard the space shuttle *Discovery* in 1998, becoming the oldest person to fly in outer space at age seventy-seven, and is one of the last surviving members of the Mercury Seven.

---

Emily Brontë (July 30, 1818–December 19, 1848) was a British novelist and poet. She is most often remembered for her only novel, *Wuthering Heights,* which is an English literature classic. She published under the masculine pen name Ellis Bell to evade contemporary prejudice against female writers.

Facilitate students' understanding that intellectual strength is another way of describing tenacity or the specific talents, abilities, and skills a person possesses and continually uses. Relate the concept of intellectual strength to personal achievement or the attainment of goals as a consequence of the trait of tenacity.

Discuss how social, technological, economic, and political ⊿ trends affect the display and appreciation of a person's tenacity.

## ACTIVATE PRIOR KNOWLEDGE

Review the meaning of attributes, traits, and characteristics.

Describe how attributes can define intellectual strengths and how intellectual strengths are identified: tests, work samples, performances, opinions, or judgments by knowledgeable observers. Provide a set of scenarios wherein students can discern an individual's intellectual strength(s).

| |
|---|
| Carlos picked up a pencil and began to "scribble" on the paper while he was waiting for his mother to finish shopping. A person walked by him and said, "My gosh, that's an outstanding picture." "Thanks," said Carlos. "It's just a scribble." |
| Melissa wrapped her report about ants in a beautiful piece of paper. She wrote a note to her grandmother wishing her a "Happy Birthday." She gave her report to her grandmother because she wanted her to see what the teacher had written on the cover of her report: *Your work about ants is excellent. Maybe you should consider becoming an entomologist.* |

Use these "intellectual snapshots" to prompt discussions about the definition, exhibition, and consequence of using and recognizing intellectual strength.

Discuss how each person's intellectual strengths form the total composition of the individual by having students compile a "strengths" chart illustrating their own intellectual strengths.

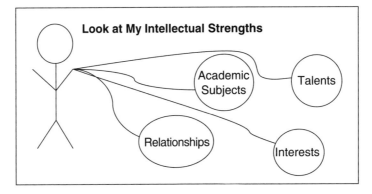

**Look at My Intellectual Strengths**

Academic Subjects

Talents

Relationships

Interests

## RELATIONSHIP TO PCM

## Core Curriculum

Present characters from literature or history students have previously studied and instruct them to *both* identify and justify the "intellectual strengths" of these people or their ability to use their potential.

Create a class chart to synthesize the various illustrations of intellectual strengths. (Note the example included on the chart.)

| Individuals | Intellectual Strength(s) | Evidence | Outcomes |
|---|---|---|---|
| Abraham Lincoln | Stated clearly a belief | Written speech | Changed people's behavior |
|  |  |  |  |
|  |  |  |  |

## Curriculum of Practice

Conduct a real or imaginary interview by mail, telephone, or email to investigate how a selected person in a specialized field used one or more of their intellectual strengths to fulfill a task.

Provide students with a list of key questions for the interview:

## Interview Questions

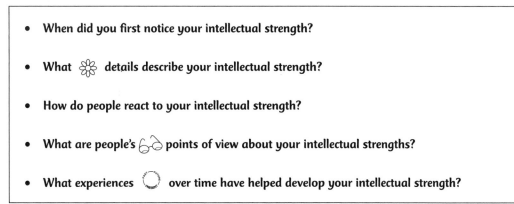

- When did you first notice your intellectual strength?

- What ✽ details describe your intellectual strength?

- How do people react to your intellectual strength?

- What are people's 👓 points of view about your intellectual strengths?

- What experiences ⟳ over time have helped develop your intellectual strength?

Share the students' data from interviews to identify common ✽ details and ⚛ patterns about the use of intellectual strengths.

## Curriculum of Connections

Provide students with an opportunity to discuss the following 🏛 big idea:

> ### Intellectual ability can be viewed as positive and/or negative.

Encourage students to use the information collected about characters in literature or history to "take a position" on this statement and participate in a discussion or debate.

Have students write an autobiography to describe how an intellectual strength can become an asset or liability in different contexts or situations. Introduce contexts or situations that are academic as well as personal.

## Curriculum of Identity

Present students with actions that are recognized outcomes of using intellectual strengths:

- Solve complex problems
- Anticipate or contribute to the future
- Summarize and apply new or different information
- Provide an alternate idea

Instruct students to describe how these actions influence the ⚛ patterns of behavior defined in historical "heroes and heroines."

## LESSON G: RECEPTIVITY TO EXPERIENCE

**PCM Focus:** Receptivity to experience

**Objective:** Students will develop an understanding of how to become receptive to learning experiences by assuming specific cognitive and affective behaviors.

## MOTIVATE

Present the following poster to the students. Discuss the types of senses and their use for learning.

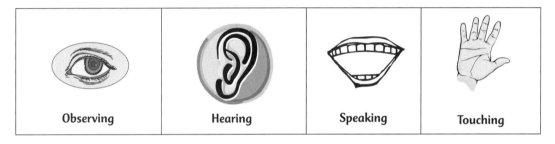

| Observing | Hearing | Speaking | Touching |

Ask students to match the following activities to the senses most relevant to them.

- Learning about rocks
- Learning to draw
- Learning about history by reading a book
- Learning about music

## ACTIVATE PRIOR KNOWLEDGE

Make an analogy between constructing a puzzle and learning something new.

Cut out and use a set of puzzle pieces to illustrate kinesthetically how new learning fits into existing knowledge or learning.

Practice the concept with examples relevant to what students have learned and will learn. Underscore the fact that prior knowledge relates to or clarifies new information by making connections.

| New Learning | Previous Learning | The Relationship |
|---|---|---|
| We will learn new things about Mars. | We know that explorers found or discovered a New World. | Explorations give new information. |
| | | |

## RELATIONSHIP TO PCM

### Core Curriculum

Introduce the skill set important to becoming a receptive learner or student.

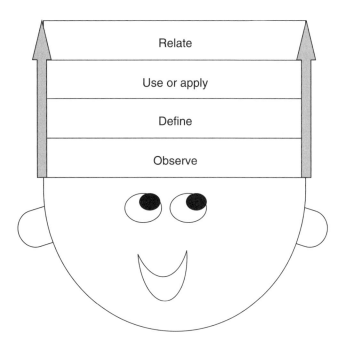

Describe and exemplify the ☙ language of the discipline or the meaning of each skill:

- Relate: connect, link
- Use or apply: practice
- Define: describe
- Observe: look at

Discuss the importance of the skill set to developing receptivity or interest and to the willingness to learn. Practice the skill set while learning something new.

### Curriculum of Practice

Introduce students to how scholars develop the art of viewing things from 👓 multiple perspectives by observing a painting in a museum as an example.

Stand to the side to view the picture.

Stand close and in front of the picture.

Stand far back to view the picture.

Discuss how different distances from the same object affect your perception of ✿ details and ⚛ patterns. Research how 👓 a point of view affects what people learn and know in different disciplines or areas of study.

## Curriculum of Connections and Identity

Instruct students to observe the "Growth of an Idea" in a selected discipline.

| Growth of an Idea in: _____ | | | | |
|---|---|---|---|---|
| First | Second | Third | Fourth | And then |
| | | | | |

Use a specific example illustrating the chronology of an idea to describe how and why "receptivity to experience" is a valuable contribution to becoming personally accomplished or academically successful.

# 2

# Participation Skills

## LESSON A: QUESTIONING

**PCM Focus:** Questioning

**Objective:** Students will be able to participate in discussions and other types of learning experiences by developing the skill of questioning.

## MOTIVATE

List the importance of practicing the "art of questioning" on a chart. (Note that the following learning experience is completed in segments.)

1. Use the chart to define the relevance of questioning in these situations:

| Practicing Questioning | | | |
|---|---|---|---|
| Getting lost | Forgetting something you knew | Meeting something unfamiliar or new | Wanting to understand something |

2. Discuss the affective responses when people feel the need to ask questions:

| Affective Responses to Questioning | | | |
|---|---|---|---|
| Proud | Embarrassed | Clever or creative | Hesitant |

3. Use both strips (Practicing Questioning) and (Affective Responses to Questioning) to *match* the need to ask questions to the responses individuals have when questioning. For example, getting lost could be embarrassing.

Ask students to describe a ✦ pattern about asking and responding to questions. Define the ◆ ethics of questioning in different contexts as a consequence of this activity.

## ACTIVATE PRIOR KNOWLEDGE

Define the differences between being a *questioner* and a *respondent*: the questioner forms and asks the question, and the respondent answers a question.

Have students list situations in which they assume the roles of respondent or questioner.

| Situations | Roles | |
|---|---|---|
| | Questioner | Respondent |
| | | |
| | | |
| | | |
| | | |

Use the chart to reveal a relationship between situations and the roles students assume as questioners and respondents.

Introduce the concepts of being an active versus passive participant in different situations. Provide students with a subject-specific situation and instruct them to define their role as active or passive in each situation and to describe why they are assuming the role they've chosen.

| Look at Me | | |
|---|---|---|
| Situations | Active Role | Passive Role |
| Mathematics | | |
| Science | | |
| Social Studies | | |
| Language Arts | | |

Discuss the implications of 👓 perceiving oneself as an active versus passive learner.

Discuss the information depicted on the "Look at Me" chart as a means of viewing a "portrait of the self as a learner."

## RELATIONSHIP TO PCM

### Core Curriculum

Introduce and reinforce the value of asking questions in becoming a "scholar."

Present the keywords chart to prompt forming questions in any academic setting or endeavor.

# Forming Questions

| This | and | this | equals | Question |
|------|-----|------|--------|----------|
| Who | | reasons | | _____? |
| What | | kinds | | _____? |
| Where | | consequence | | _____? |
| When | | conditions | | _____? |
| Why | | significant | | _____? |
| How | | purposes | | _____? |

Facilitate the practice of questioning by using the keywords on the chart as a stimulus. Example: to ask about weather, students could form a question by matching **what** to **conditions:** *What are the weather conditions today?*

## Curriculum of Practice

Introduce the concepts of open or divergent and closed or convergent questions.

Define the purposes behind forming and using these types of questions.

Emphasize the appropriate use of open versus closed questions in various contexts using the following list of learning episodes:

- Needing a reference
- Wanting an explanation
- Clarifying a complicated idea
- Requiring many possible ways of performing a task

Facilitate students' understanding of open (divergent) and closed (convergent) questions by asking them to form ⬚ rules about question types and techniques.

Select discipline(s) students can investigate to determine the types of questions most prevalent in the pursuit of knowledge in the discipline(s) and ask them to summarize their findings about question usage in the discipline(s).

## Using Questions in the Disciplines

| Discipline | Knowledge Sought | Question Preference |
|---|---|---|
| Example: Physiology | Purpose of the circulatory system | Closed |
| Example: Physiology | Importance of oxygen to the body | Open |
| | | |
| | | |

## Curriculum of Connections

Introduce the 🏛 big idea:

### The quest for knowledge is dependent on the art of questioning.

Discuss the 👓 multiple perspectives about this statement.

Provide students with the option to "take a position" regarding the efficacy of the 🏛 big idea.

Instruct the students to relate the 🏛 big idea to a selected group of people comprised of an inventor, author, and historical figure.

Ask the students to use the chart to analyze the 🏛 big idea given the information they have discovered about the people they researched.

### The quest for knowledge is dependent on the art of questioning.

| People | Accomplishments | Types of Questions Used |
|---|---|---|
| Inventor | | |
| Scientist | | |
| Historical figure | | |

## Curriculum of Identity

Provide students with a synopsis of Socrates's questioning techniques. Ask them to use the synopsis in formulating their own philosophy of questioning to be delivered in an essay.

## The Socratic Method

Socrates (470–399 BC) was a Greek philosopher who, despite being considered one of the greatest and most important philosophers who ever lived, left no writings at all. Most of what we know about his life and work comes from the writings of his disciples, Xenophon and Plato. He lived during a period of transition in the Greek Empire, and after the Peloponnesian War, he was tried, convicted, and executed for corrupting the young.

Socrates engaged in the questioning of his students in an unending search for truth. He sought to get to the foundations of his students' and colleagues' views by asking continual questions until a contradiction was exposed, thus proving the fallacy of the initial assumption. This type of questioning became known as the *Socratic Method* and may be Socrates's most enduring contribution to philosophy.

## LESSON B: ASKING FOR CLARIFICATION

**PCM Focus:** Asking for clarification

**Objective:** Students will be able to understand the value of asking for clarification or seeking the specific meaning of or directions to perform a task or learn something.

## MOTIVATE

Provide students with a set of directions that are deliberately unclear. Use the following script:

Boys and girls (class), you are going to draw an object. Follow my directions:
First, draw a curvy line that goes up and down.
Second, draw the same line that goes up and down on the other side.
Third, draw a line that makes it whole at the bottom.
Fourth, draw a big circle at the top.

Present the students with a completed drawing (a vase):

Prompt a discussion as to why the students' pictures are not exactly like the vase (picture) the teacher exhibits. List some of the students' reasons:

- Your directions weren't clear.
- We couldn't ask questions.
- You wouldn't repeat the directions.
- You didn't show us what to do.

Reinforce the consequences to the students themselves and to the quality of the completed task because the students were not able to ask or seek clarification. Ask students to define a ⬚ rule related to the need and purpose of asking for clarification.

Initiate a discussion as to why individuals *do not* ask or seek clarification:

- Temerity
- Self-consciousness
- Fear of letting others know they don't understand (exposure)
- Unable to form an appropriate question
- Embarrassment

## ACTIVATE PRIOR KNOWLEDGE

Introduce three characterizations of students needing clarification.

| | | |
|---|---|---|
| Will not ask for clarification (I have no questions). | Timidly asks for clarification (I have a question, but I'm scared to ask it). | Asks questions all the time even if clarifications are not needed. |

Discuss the implications of these three characterizations on learning using the following chart.

| Characteristic | Positive Effect | Negative Effect |
|---|---|---|
| Will not ask for clarification | | |
| Timidly asks for clarification | | |
| Asks for clarification all the time | | |

Identify the ⚬⚬ patterns of learning that occur when these characterizations are exhibited by students.

## RELATIONSHIP TO PCM

### Core Curriculum

Select an excerpt from the various disciplines or subject areas: social studies, language arts, math, and science. Present the excerpt, as in the following examples, to the class:

# Number 1: Science

Dolphins, whales, and *sea* cows live under water for their whole lives. Blubber helps them keep warm. They breathe air through a blowhole. They come to the surface to get air through their blowhole.

# Number 2: Social Studies

In the mid-nineteenth century, goods such as tea, silk, and ivory were transported from the Far East. Many vessels carried these goods across vast bodies of water.

Introduce a coding system to the students: An _____ (underline) represents clearly understood information; a ⬭ (circle) represents information that requires clarity or demands asking for clarification.

Instruct students to read the excerpt and code it. Discuss *how* and *why* the students will ask for clarification and discuss the purposes of clarification, that is, to provide understanding and to remember the information.

Here is an example from the sample excerpts:

> Number 1: Blubber could be information requiring clarification. Number 2: Vessels could be information requiring clarification.

Summarize the learning experience by asking why different people identify different things needing clarification.

## Curriculum of Practice

Present and discuss the list of methods or procedures by which scholars seek clarification. Discuss the 👄 language of the discipline, which is necessary to seek clarification.

## Seeking Clarification

| Method | Discipline or Topic Usage Examples |
|---|---|
| Asking questions | |
| Examining the parts of the whole | |
| Drawing a picture | |
| Conducting research | |
| Discussing with someone else | |
| Matching or connecting one idea to another | |
| Magnifying or enlarging | |

Encourage students to select a discipline or topic within a discipline to uncover how each method to gain clarity is used in that selected discipline or topic.

## Curriculum of Connections

Introduce the 🏛 big idea:

## Ideas are illuminated in different ways.

Discuss the word "illuminate" as related to the meaning of "seeking clarification."

Instruct students to apply the 🏛 big idea to various discipline-specific situations: language arts (the definition of a colloquial saying, for example, "It's awesome"); science (defining differences between forms of energy); social studies (describing a historic event); mathematics (defining the value of a sum). Use the chart to categorize information from the various disciplines that exemplify the 🏛 big idea.

## Support It ...

## 🏛 Ideas are illuminated in different ways.

| Discipline | | |
|---|---|---|
| Example | | |

## Curriculum of Identity

Present the "Wheel of Clarification" by introducing the middle circle describing how people feel when they are not clear about a task or learning experience.

Introduce the outside circle defining the ways people can seek clarification. Have students align the inside to the outside wheels as a way to illustrate how seeking clarification can be resolved by exhibiting a specific behavior.

Apply the wheel to specific class-related learning experiences: writing a story, learning to multiply, and so on. Students could keep the wheel in their desks as a reminder of ways to attain clarification when learning.

## LESSON C: RESTATING

**PCM Focus:** Restating

**Objective:** Students will be able to comprehend the significance of restating what has been learned in their own words in order to verify and confirm their understanding of content or skills.

## MOTIVATE

Say something to the class in a jumbled, sophisticated manner or in another language. Ask the students why the communication was unclear and needs to be restated in another form. Here are some examples:

- We are going to assimilate the information in its original jargon and context. (We need to learn it in the right language and situation.)
- ¿Que hora es? (What time is it?)

Inform the students that they are going to be introduced to some idioms that they are to restate in their own words:

- It's a piece of cake.
- Don't cry over spilled milk.
- Keep an eye on him/her.
- It's a small world.
- Practice makes perfect.

Discuss why the skill of restating is related to learning the following skills:

- Justifying
- Confirming
- Authenticating
- Verifying
- Seeking truth

## ACTIVATE PRIOR KNOWLEDGE

Discuss times in and out of school when restating was required to achieve meaning.

| Times When | | |
|---|---|---|
| | **Situations** | **Need for Restating** |
| At school | | |
| At home | | |
| At play | | |

Discuss the value of role-playing, or how an "enactment" of a situation is a way to restate a problem or event and is a helpful tool to learn and/or comprehend.

Present the following scenarios as a way to illustrate or demonstrate when and how to restate in order to enhance meaning.

| Scenario 1 | | |
|---|---|---|
| **What Was Said** | **Asking to Restate** | **The New Statement** |
| The text says, "Weather determines the flight patterns and landing of the space shuttle." | Student asks, "What do we mean by the idea of weather? It is very general." | Stormy weather can determine the flight pattern and landing of the space shuttle. |

| Scenario 2 | | |
|---|---|---|
| **What Was Said** | **Asking to Restate** | **The New Statement** |
| The picture of animals in the forest had dark and thick wavy lines over the head of the zebra. | Student asks: "What are the lines suppose to represent?" | Dark and thick wavy lines were used by the artist to indicate danger near the zebra. |

Ask students to respond to the sections of the scenario that (1) ask for a restatement and (2) define or describe the restatement. Note from the example that the generality of a phrase is restated with specific ❀ detail.

Emphasize the fact that there are 👓 multiple points of view regarding how to ask for a restatement and how the restatement can be formalized.

Compare the skill of restating to other skills:

- restate—repeat
- restate—reorganize
- restate—translate
- restate—reword

Name all the situations related to learning that require the skill of restating:

- Learning a foreign language
- Emphasizing a point
- Helping someone understand something

Have students name the ⬡ patterns that reflect the opportunities and/or need to restate.

## RELATIONSHIP TO PCM

### Core Curriculum

Discuss that restating must be consistent or faithful to the original communication to prevent "distortion of the original or truth" of the message.

Relate the game of "Telephone" to maintaining fidelity in restating information, communications, and/or messages.

Select an historical event, and instruct students to research the same event in multiple print and nonprint sources. Describe the purpose of this activity as identifying how restating even in academic work can affect the meaning and truth of an historical event.

Define how "restating" is an integral feature of describing history and can have negative and positive effects.

### Curriculum of Practice

Introduce the study of epistemology as the branch of philosophy that examines knowledge and the extent it can be certain or probable.

Trace an idea related to science from its inception to its current presentation. Determine the degree to which the process of restating has maintained or distorted the understanding of the idea.

### Curriculum of Connections

Discuss the nature and purposes of conducting a survey using a questionnaire. Provide examples of when and why surveys have been conducted and the benefits derived from analyzing survey data.

Describe political, social, and economic trends that cause surveys to be conducted.

- Election preferences
- Product development and satisfaction
- Entertainment favorites or ratings

Facilitate the students in forming a set of questions to survey peers (and adults) regarding a specific issue. Determine why questions on the survey may need to be restated to be comprehensible to different audiences.

- Why do people need to have something restated?
- How can people provide a restatement of the original idea?
- When is restating beneficial?

Conduct the survey.

Synthesize the data from the survey to identify both the ⛬ rules for conducting a survey and the ⚛ patterns and related ❁ details obtained.

Decide how to restate the data from the survey to make it accessible to different audiences.

## Curriculum of Identity

Describe the purposes of "before" and "after" pictures.

Instruct students to portray themselves *before* and *after* the process of asking for and receiving a restatement of a communication.

| Before Restating | After Restating |
|---|---|
|  |  |

## LESSON D: ACKNOWLEDGING PEERS

**PCM Focus:** Acknowledging peers

**Objective:** Students will be able to understand that becoming a member of a group can be achieved by developing techniques that include empathy for, acceptance of, and respect of peers in the group.

## MOTIVATE

Introduce behaviors that exemplify how people acknowledge each other's accomplishments, work, and contributions:

- Smiling
- Applause
- Giving flowers
- Presenting an award
- Complimenting

Discuss why these patterns of behavior are analogous to a stimulus or way to engage interaction between and among people.

Introduce the Acknowledgment Chart and describe its multiple and varied uses in promoting acceptance for and support to other people in and out of school situations.

### Acknowledgment Chart

**A**—Ask a question related to what the peer is saying.

**C**—Comment on a behavior, skill, or work of a peer.

**K**—Kindly correct a peer.

**N**—Nod in approval to a comment by the peer.

**O**—Overtly admire a peer's work, skill, or behavior.

**W**—Wink in approval to a peer.

**L**—Laugh with a peer. Laud a peer's work.

**E**—Enthusiastically comment on a peer's work.

**D**—Describe why you liked a peer's skills, behavior, or work.

**G**—Give a peer a handshake or hug in regard to something they have accomplished.

**E**—Eye your peer as they are commenting or sharing.

Refer to the chart within the context of a lesson to prompt students' responses to a peer's work, comment, behavior, or skill. Here is an example: *Sara, what would you like to say to Danny about his response to the question?*

## ACTIVATE PRIOR KNOWLEDGE

Discuss the meaning of "reciprocal behavior" and apply it to situations at school where a student wishes another student to acknowledge him or her in the same way the student would acknowledge others.

- Getting a math problem correct
- Receiving an A on a report
- Having a picture hanging on a bulletin board
- Running at a handball game

Conduct a discussion to define the meaning of the statement "acknowledging others is a way of acknowledging oneself."

Use Maslow's (1970) Hierarchy of Needs to further understand the pervasive need of people to "belong."

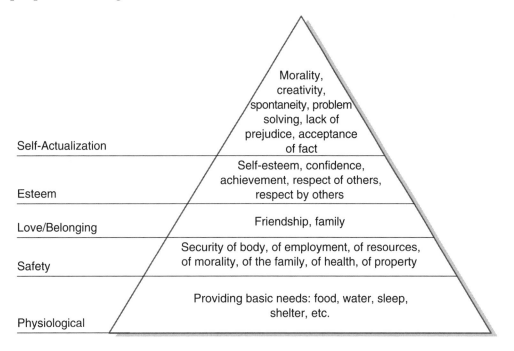

Discuss how becoming a member of a group (belonging) is an important part of "a community of learners" and "a democratic classroom."

Discuss the ◆ ethical issues that emerge from situations where people acknowledge others.

## RELATIONSHIP TO PCM

### Core Currriculum

Introduce a collection of comments that reflect 👓 multiple perceptions of how people acknowledge the work or accomplishments of others:

- Good job!
- Wow, I wish I could do work like that.
- Could you show me how to do that as well as you did it?
- I want you to be my teacher.
- That's the best I've seen!

Instruct students to read fiction or nonfiction selections to find specific examples of how individuals or groups have acknowledged others for their "good" work.

### Curriculum of Practice

Present the concept that peer-to-peer collaborative learning is a forum for acknowledging peers. Discuss how peers can be a source for learning in a variety of situations:

- Lecture
- Conference
- Conversation
- Seminar
- Discussion (in person or online)
- Exhibition
- Chat room

Provide students with a fictitious conference program such as what follows to review and validate how peers can learn from each other.

### Space Age Conference

- General Session: Another Voyage to the Moon
- Panel Discussion: The Price of Space Travel
- Seminar: Training Astronauts at NASA
- Film or Video Series: What Happened to Pluto?
- Closing Speech: What We Know About Mars

Instruct the students to research journals and newspaper articles for examples of how professionals or scholars have learned from each other.

Define the political, social, and economic 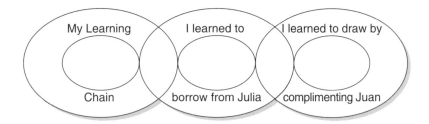 trends influencing when and why peers learn from each other.

## Curriculum of Connections

Introduce the 🏛 big idea:

> ### The power to learn can be affected by acknowledging peers.

Research situations in history when people have learned from peers after acknowledging their accomplishments or achievements. Note the following examples:

- What did Orwell and Wilbur Wright learn from each other?
- What did Louis Pasteur's peers learn from him?
- What did Buzz Aldrin's peers learn from him?

Synthesize the discussion by helping students understand the value of acknowledgment as integral to the process of peer-to-peer learning, innovation, and progress.

## Curriculum of Identity

Construct a "peer-to-peer learning chain" to illustrate how acknowledging a peer forms a link in the learning chain.

# 3

# Self-Advocacy

## LESSON A: ESTABLISHING A VOICE

**PCM Focus:** Establishing a voice

**Objective:** Students will be able to appreciate why establishing a voice or assuming a point of view is significant to the individual.

## MOTIVATE

Introduce the concept of "voice" by determining how different "things" have their own voices.

### What's My Voice?

Discuss the 🏛 big idea:

## Everyone has a voice.

Discuss the distinguishing features of a voice: a means of expression, choice, opinion.

## ACTIVATE PRIOR KNOWLEDGE

Define the concept of voice for each individual shown in these situations:

Present students with a continuum illustrating the intensity of how people represent their voices in situations that demand a 👓 point of view.

| Least Supportive | Undecided to Support | Most Supportive |
|---|---|---|
|  |  |  |

Discuss the differences among the various terms used to express 👓 point of view (Least Supportive, Undecided to Support, and Most Supportive). Identify ideas or 👓 points of view from a story, current event, and classroom or playground situation. Have students practice "taking a stand" and then identifying the place on the continuum that reflects the intensity of their 👓 point of view.

Present a school-related issue (lost books, too much noise in the cafeteria, etc.) and "create the voice" to respond to the situation. Instruct students that in these contexts, "VOICE" is heard and represents a definitive opinion.

| Situation | Voice |
|---|---|
|  |  |

## RELATIONSHIP TO PCM

### Core Curriculum

Discuss the multiple occasions in history when people have spoken "with one voice." Create a quasi–time line to provide a historical context to describe when people have expressed themselves with one voice.

| Listen to Us: A Time Line | | | |
|---|---|---|---|
|  |  |  |  |

## Curriculum of Practice

Discuss why and how people have established their voice. Explore the idea that "voices have been heard and have caused change."

Research people whose voices made a difference.

Trace how and why these people established their voices.

Share the researched information to determine the commonalities among people who establish a voice.

## Curriculum of Connections

Present a controversial situation derived from literature, history, or school. Instruct students to develop their voice in response to the posed situation.

Use elements such as vision and clarity of purpose to establish a voice about a school-related issue to be shared in the classroom.

## Curriculum of Identity

Select a community or social issue to develop a campaign that will include a position paper reflecting the student's voice regarding the issue.

Discuss the many ways students have changed the course of events, using their voices for social action.

## LESSON B: BUILDING CONFIDENCE

**PCM Focus:** Building confidence

**Objective:** Students will be able to recognize and employ the skills related to becoming confident in a learning situation.

## MOTIVATE

Present students with these separate "bricks" depicting the concept of confidence.

Sticking to the Task

Achieving Some Success

Getting Assistance to Learn More

Doing Something Successfully

Practicing to Know Something Well

Gaining Recognition for Doing Something Well

Discuss each of the "bricks to build confidence" and how they relate to becoming confident.

Present a fictitious character and use the attributes of this character to match to the traits of building confidence defined on the bricks.

Gene the Giant was terrified. Everyone thought that giants could lift even a huge tree with one big tug. However, Gene the Giant didn't feel strong and felt he couldn't even lift a plant or even a small tree. How can he build his confidence?

## ACTIVATE PRIOR KNOWLEDGE

Ask students to reflect on previous school experiences when they felt a lack of confidence or the need to build confidence to succeed at tasks or learning experiences. Compare these experiences to times or situations when they exhibited confidence in the tasks.

| Building Confidence | |
| --- | --- |
| **Situations Lacking Confidence** | **Situations Feeling Confident** |
| | |
| | |
| **My Confidence Profile** | |
| | |

Ask students to use the completed chart to identify the ⚯ patterns of behavior related to using and building confidence. Have students describe their Confidence Profile.

## RELATIONSHIP TO PCM

### Core Curriculum

Trace the achievements of a literary or historical character to prove or disprove this 🏛 big idea:

### Self-confidence is a consequence of achievement.

### Curriculum of Practice

Review the following prompts of depth and complexity and define them with respect to the concept of confidence.

| Terms | Relationship to Building Confidence | Application to Learning Subjects at School |
| --- | --- | --- |
| ✽ Details | | |
| ⚯ Patterns | | |

| ⊟ Rules | Confidence can be built by learning and following rules. | The rules give information on how to write a story and help you feel confident to do the work. |
|---|---|---|
| ◆ Ethics | | |
| ◯ Over time | | |
| 👓 Points of view | | |

Use the chart to illustrate the role "building confidence" has in learning. (Note the one completed example on the chart.)

## Curriculum of Connections

Introduce this 🏛 big idea:

> # Having confidence is situational.

Discuss the meaning of the 🏛 big idea and the ramifications of its meaning for individuals at different ages, for learning different subject areas, for belonging to different groups, and for experiencing different types of success.

Consider conducting this task with references about noted heroes and heroines from literature or history.

## Curriculum of Identity

Have each student identify a school-based situation that warrants a need to build his or her confidence. Instruct students to outline the skills they will use to build their confidence with regard to participating in the situation.

## LESSON C: ESTABLISHING AN IDENTITY

**PCM Focus:** Establishing an identity

**Objective:** Each student will be able to define himself or herself as a learner in multiple contexts.

## MOTIVATE

Present the students with a collection of photographs or well-noted brand names, symbols, or insignias that *identify* the object.

Write the word *identify* on a chart or board to prompt discussion about its meaning. Insert dictionary definitions and thesaurus synonyms to stimulate further conversation.

Summarize the value of an identity to people as well as products.

Discuss how an individual forms an identity:

- Appearance
- Actions
- Achievements

## ACTIVATE PRIOR KNOWLEDGE

Analyze a set of preselected pictures of individuals, animals, and plants to name the distinctive attributes that identify them.

Add an additional set of pictures to verify and test the responses students made.

Collect the ideas generated by the students that answer this question: *How do living things develop an identity?* Note the examples on a chart.

---

### Creating an Identity

- Coloration
- Physical features or attributes
- Size
- Behavior or actions
- Experiences

---

## RELATIONSHIP TO PCM

### Core Curriculum

Review with students grade-level standards that can best reinforce the concept of identity. Here are some examples:

- *Language arts:* the use of language to identify mood and of the conventions of language identifiable as to purpose or function
- *Mathematics:* identify attributes of plane figures in geometry
- *Science:* properties of elements
- *Social studies:* branches of the government

Use the selected standards to validate the types of attributes that create an identity for these topics.

### Curriculum Practice

Define the traits or characteristics that establish an identity for a discipline and disciplinarian in that field. Note the example that astronomy and astronomers are identified by interest in and knowledge of "stars."

### Curriculum Connections

Utilize the concept of *identity* as an overarching theme or universal concept to investigate its role, purpose, and/or function across subject areas or disciplines. Examples:

- *Literature:* identity of the author's style, identity of characters
- *Mathematics:* identity of quantity, shape, and size

## Curriculum Identity

Write a brief personal narrative to this prompt, *What gives me my identity?* as the preface to the following learning experiences.

Introduce students to the segment of the fairy tale when the queen looks into the mirror and says "Mirror, mirror on the wall. Who is the fairest of them all?"

Discuss the implications of this scene: What is the answer to the question? Why would a mirror not tell the truth?

Discuss the use of mirrors and the images they cast:

- When do people look in the mirror?
- Why do people look in a mirror?
- What do they expect to see?

 Ask students to draw sketches of themselves and then to draw sketches of each other. Describe the similarities and differences of multiple perceptions. Explain how your perception of yourself and someone else's perception of you may differ. Discuss other ways or methods people can receive images of themselves.

Define this 🏛 big idea:

> # We view ourselves in relationship to or comparison with other people's view of us.

Engage students in discussing how they can be identified as a "learner." Provide students with ideas to initiate their responses:

- Me as a learner answering questions
- Me as a learner doing something "new"

## LESSON D: MULTIPLE GROUP MEMBERSHIP

**PCM Focus:** Multiple group membership

**Objective:** Students will understand and appreciate how single individuals can have multiple group memberships: cultural group membership, peer group membership, religious group membership, school group membership, and so on.

## MOTIVATE

Present the students with a box of objects to sort into different categories.

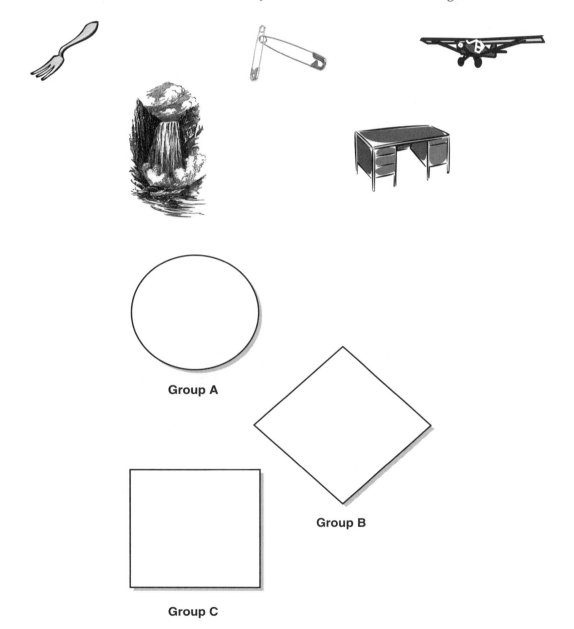

**Group A**

**Group B**

**Group C**

Require students to explain and justify the reason(s) for classifying an object into a specific group.

Ask other students to re-sort an object to illustrate how it can justifiably be a member of more than one group.

## ACTIVATE PRIOR KNOWLEDGE

Introduce the 🏛 big idea:

### Things can have multiple memberships.

Discuss the meaning of the terms *multiple* and *membership*.

Show students the diagram of overlapping circles to provide examples of a person or an object (place, or thing) that represents multiple memberships. Have students explain how the entity could have multiple memberships.

- Example:

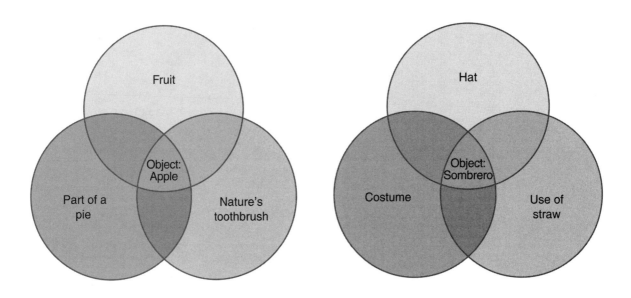

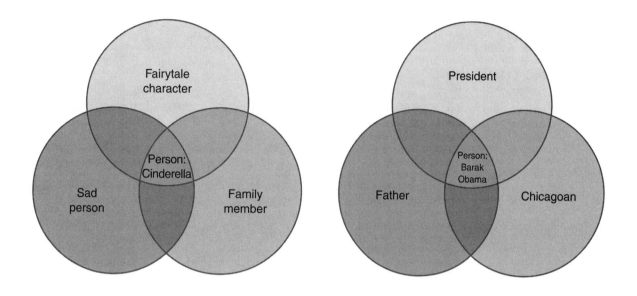

Focus the discussion on the 🏛 big idea previously introduced to the students and ask them to verify, validate, and/or authenticate the 🏛 big idea from the examples shown.

Introduce an empty diagram set of overlapping circles and instruct students to provide examples of how a single person can have multiple memberships to groups.

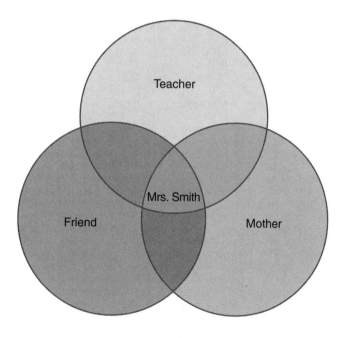

# RELATIONSHIP TO PCM

## Core Curriculum

Use the diagram to illustrate how something under study shares simultaneous membership in multiple groups.

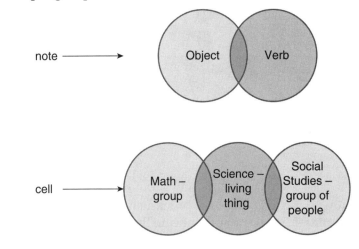

## Curriculum of Practice

Present students with the diagrams and instructions to show how the ideas or objects in one discipline have membership in other disciplines. Note the example that an idea in philosophy ("Ignorance is the only evil"—Socrates) also has membership in psychology and sociology.

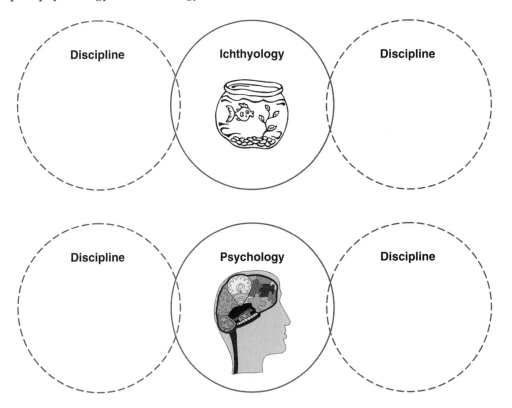

## Curriculum of Connections

Discuss how and why people prioritize their affiliations or memberships to groups.

Study a hero or heroine; describe the multiple cultures to which the person belongs and prioritize them from most to least important. Support the prioritizations with cited evidence from print materials.

| Cultural Ladder | |
|---|---|
| **Hero/Heroine:** _____ | |
| **Priority** | **Group Membership** |
| Most | |
| 3 | |
| 2 | |
| Least | |

## Curriculum of Identity

Define the many cultures to which Abraham Lincoln belonged.

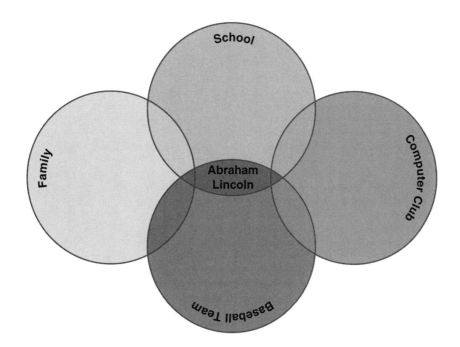

Answer these questions:

- What are the threads or links connecting the various cultures?
- What common values do the cultures share?
- Discuss how and why people prioritize their affiliations or membership among cultures.

Provide students with the opportunity to illustrate or diagram how they simultaneously are members of multiple groups or cultures. Note the teacher example:

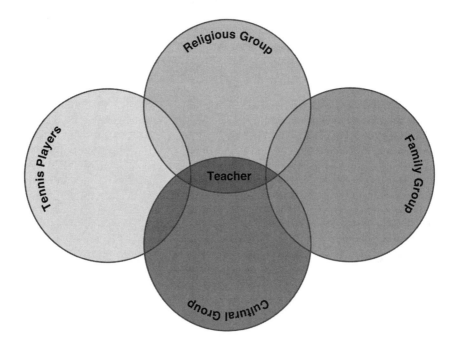

Discuss how multiple memberships is a universal trait of people.

# 4

# Presentation Skills

## Presentation Skills Matrix

| | | | |
|---|---|---|---|
| Describing from concrete<br><br>to<br><br>abstract | Showing visual clues | Using the voice to emphasize ideas | Asking closed and open questions |
| Presenting the self as confident | Maintaining focus on the topic | Maintaining eye contact with the listeners | Using words that define, describe, and explain |

# LESSON A: TALKING STEPS

**PCM Focus:** Talking steps

**Objective:** Students will identify and follow the explicit steps that form a 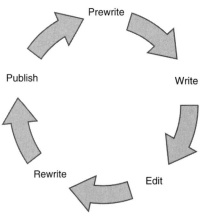 pattern to develop a presentation based on an interest from previously learned information.

## MOTIVATE

Discuss the many and varied ways people perform tasks in different settings following a specific set of steps that form a ⚬⚬ pattern.

| Home Task: | School Task: | Play Task: |
|---|---|---|
| 3 | 3 | 3 |
| 2 | 2 | 2 |
| 1 | 1 | 1 |

Discuss the positive and/or negative implications of adhering to or breaking the ⚬⚬ pattern of steps to perform a task.

## Following the ⚬⚬ Pattern of Steps to Do a Task

| Helpful | Unhelpful |
|---|---|
|  |  |

## ACTIVATE PRIOR KNOWLEDGE

Discuss the value of following the steps of the *writing process* to draft and/or formulate a composition.

Prewrite → Write → Edit → Rewrite → Publish → Prewrite

Discuss the importance and significance of adhering to the following steps for problem solving:

1. Define the problem.
2. State a hypothesis or tentative solution.
3. Gather information.
4. Develop a solution.
5. "Sell" the solution.

Identify the differences between training or practice and "academic comfort" levels as they relate to following specific steps or a 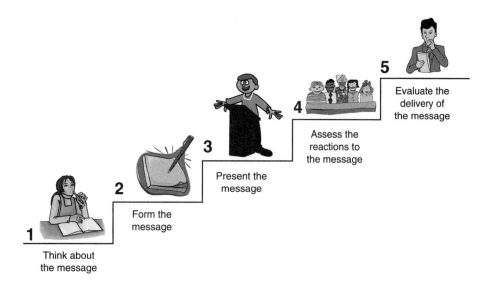 pattern to complete a task or perform a process.

## RELATIONSHIP TO PCM

## Core Curriculum

Introduce the specific "Talking Steps" included in preparing a presentation.

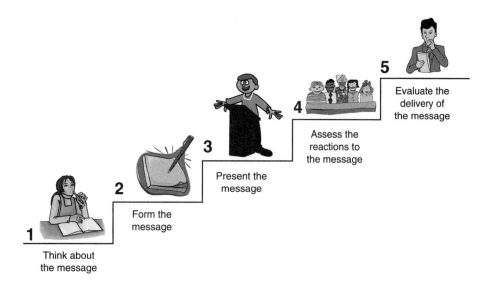

Relate the specific purposes and need for the application of the Talking Steps in the discipline-based areas that require presentation skills.

| Language Arts | Math | Science | Social Studies |
|---|---|---|---|
| Analyzing a story or book | Illustrating how a word problem was solved | Explaining how a scientific phenomenon works | Describing how a historical solution was developed |

## Curriculum of Practice

Provide students with a set of disciplines aligned with topics currently under study in the core curriculum. Have students select a disciplinarian to guide the use of the Talking Steps to develop a presentation in the topic. Note the following examples:

| Astronomy | Archeology | Statistics |
|---|---|---|
| Presentation of the appearance of various star patterns at different times of the year by an astronomer. | Presentation of the discovery of an ancient artifact by an archeologist. | Presentation of an analysis of a graph to explain a concept by a statistician. |

## Curriculum of Connections

Introduce the following 🏛 big idea:

## Presentations are an art form.

Initiate a discussion about the "art" of conducting a presentation: clarity of purpose, structure from concrete to abstract, simple to complex, part to whole, and so on.

Ask students to research people such as Bill Moyers and Diane Sawyer in the discipline of communication that have made presentations an art form. Identify the characteristics of their presentations that made them an art form.

## Curriculum of Identity

Introduce the following adjectives and their definitions (see worksheet on page 87):

- argumentative
- apathetic
- attentive
- interested
- disinterested
- agreeable
- disagreeable

Discuss how people's attitudes during a presentation affect how the presentation is received by an audience.

Discuss the behaviors students might exhibit to become more involved in conducting a presentation, lecture, or talk.

Message to Deliver

## Reading the Audience

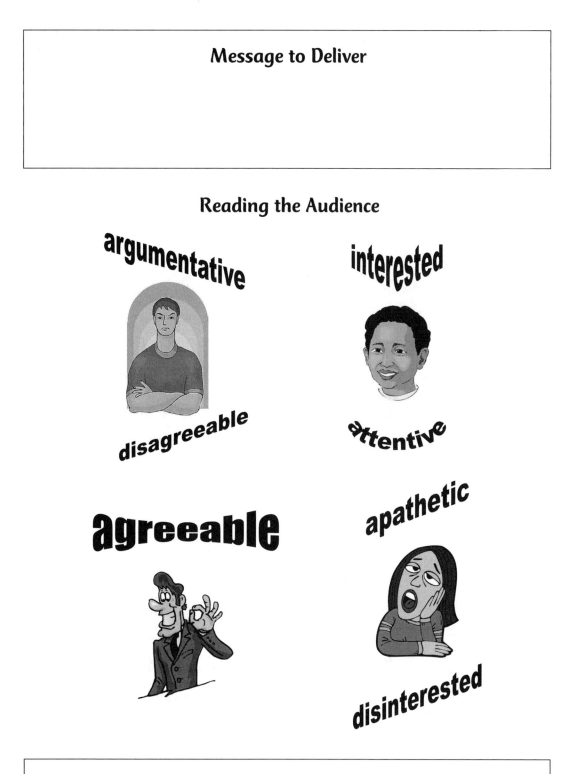

Redrafting the Communication to Meet Audience Needs

## LESSON B: WAYS TO SAY IT

**PCM Focus:** *Ways to say it*

**Objective:** *Students will be able to match various modes of delivering a "message" or communicative presentation to the type of message and situation or context.*

## MOTIVATE

Define the many similarities and differences to understand and respond to the same message in different forms of communication.

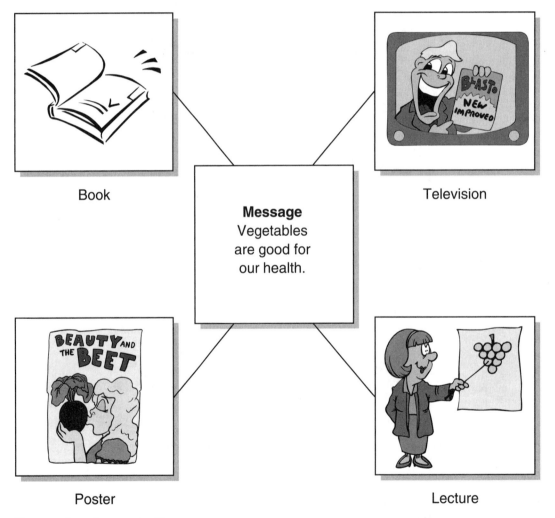

Book

Television

**Message**
Vegetables
are good for
our health.

Poster

Lecture

Respond to these questions:

- What is the relationship between the message and the media that communicates it?
- How does the way a message is sent affect how it is received by the individual?

## ACTIVATE PRIOR KNOWLEDGE

Show students how different forms of communication assume different meanings in different situations or contexts. Ask students to determine how effectively they believe the message matches the situation or context in the following pictures. Discuss what could be changed to deliver a better or more effective message.

A billboard
message on a
very busy street.

A television
message shown
very late at night.

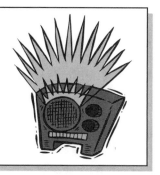

A radio message
heard in a dark
crowded room.

## RELATIONSHIP TO PCM

### Core Curriculum

Introduce the worksheet "Ways to Say It," on p. 93, by defining and exemplifying each section.

1. *Communicate a message:* This area defines the information to be shared with others.

2. *Situation or context:* This area identifies the time and place for the information to be communicated. Some places are formal such as at the school or at a special meeting. Some places are informal such as where two friends hold a conversation.

3. *Options for delivery:* This area refers to the media or form used to share information:
   - technology
   - games
   - drawings or illustrations
   - dramatizations
   - charts
   - lecture

4. *Selected responses:* This area refers to the types of reactions the presenter communicating anticipates or wants to receive from the audience. Considering audience responses helps us shape or select our "options for delivery."

5. *What to consider next:* This area helps the communicator determine how to actually adjust the presentation of information to the audience.

Select a standards-based topic that has been studied and use it as the basis to design a presentation using the "Ways to Say It" worksheet (see page 91) as a template for the activity.

## Curriculum of Practice

Instruct students to read and respond to the following letter from a disciplinarian or specialist in a field:

Dear students,

I am a geologist who has a very large and exotic collection of rocks and books and posters about these rocks. I would very much like to share or present these to your school. However, I want to make sure that they will be presented to the students in a form that will be exciting and capture their attention. Please tell me how to deliver this presentation and when and where you think the presentation should be made.

Sincerely,
Dr. Rocke

## Curriculum of Connections

Discuss the implications of the following 🏛 big idea:

### The time and place for a presentation affects how it will be delivered.

Select a previously studied topic about which students need or want to communicate.

Ask students to match the selected topic to a context (time and place) for its specific form of presentation and explain the rationale for their choices.

Discuss why and how different forms of delivery can be used to present the same information in different contexts.

# Ways to Say It

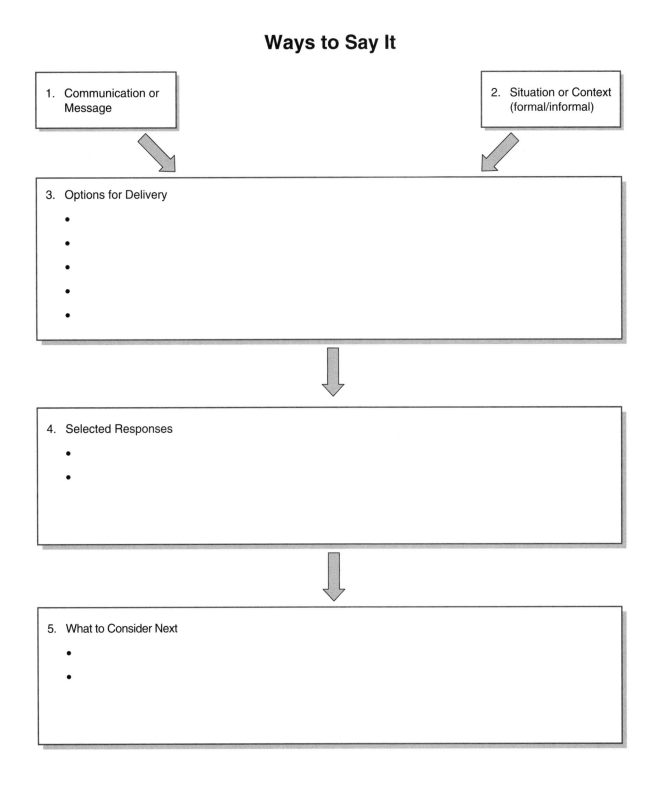

1. Communication or Message

2. Situation or Context (formal/informal)

3. Options for Delivery

- 
- 
- 
- 
- 

4. Selected Responses

- 
- 

5. What to Consider Next

- 
-

| Topic to Be Presented: _____ | | |
|---|---|---|
| **Contexts (times and places)** | **Forms of Delivery** | **Effects on the Communication** |
| Early-morning meeting of students in an auditorium | | |
| Late-afternoon meeting of students in a small room | | |
| Afternoon meeting of parents in an outdoor area. | | |

## Curriculum of Identity

Engage students in a discussion regarding their 👓 point of view about the following statement:

> ### How people appear when they present does not always match how they feel when they present.

Discuss the implications of this statement for (a) the presenter and (b) the audience.

Introduce the "How I Feel ⟵⟶ How I Want to Appear" worksheet, found on p. 93.

Discuss how and why the feelings depicted emerge and can be explained.

Discuss why it is important to disguise or "cover up" some feelings while giving a presentation.

## How I Feel ←——————→ How I Want to Appear

Scared

Relaxed

Unknowing

Knowing

Self-conscious or
uncomfortable

Proud

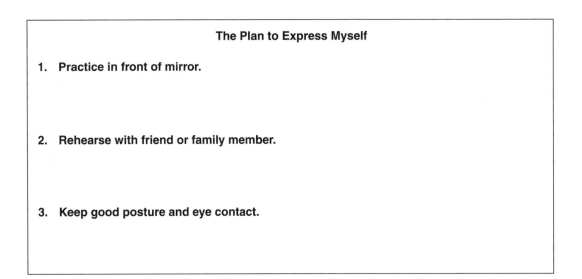

**The Plan to Express Myself**

1. **Practice in front of mirror.**

2. **Rehearse with friend or family member.**

3. **Keep good posture and eye contact.**

## LESSON C: ENGAGING THE AUDIENCE

**PCM Focus**: Engaging the audience

**Objective:** Students will be able to develop a set of strategies that facilitate peer interest and participation when they present information in a formal or informal setting.

## MOTIVATE

Make a list of *all* the ways students have seen presenters capture the attention of their audience from any venue: on a stage, on a television program, at an amusement park, at a concert, in a film, and so on.

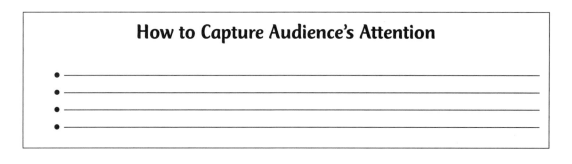

**How to Capture Audience's Attention**

- _____
- _____
- _____
- _____

Facilitate the discussion so that students recognize strategies such as:

- Soliciting questions
- Using humor
- Asking for affirmation or challenging an idea
- Requesting responses to ideas, riddles, etc.
- Using graphic art or music as a background

## ACTIVATE PRIOR KNOWLEDGE

Explain the ways in which the following forms of communication grab our attention and involvement.

Demonstration                    Explanation                    Observation

## RELATIONSHIP TO PCM

### Core Curriculum

Discuss the relationship of engagement or "attention getting" to the study of a subject and the prompts of depth and complexity. Use the following chart as a gauge to depict the degree of "attention-getting" behavior for the topic and prompt. (Note the example.)

| Topic | Prompt | Degree of "Attention Getting" | | |
| --- | --- | --- | --- | --- |
| | | None | Some | A lot |
| Example: Weather | (graph) trends | | | X |
| | | | | |
| | | | | |

### Curriculum of Practice

Discuss the figurative meaning and implications of "placing yourself in someone else's shoes."

Provide students with pictures of shoes that depict different disciplines.

Ask students to imagine wearing the shoes of the disciplinarian and to describe how they would deliver a message that engages or grabs the attention of the listener/audience.

Discuss the positive and negative consequences of using attention-getting strategies to deliver different subject matter.

### Curriculum of Connections

Conduct a debate or argue the 👓 perspective that attention-getting strategies or devices can be considered rude or impolite in some situations. For example, students sometimes gain attention by inappropriately laughing at an event.

## Curriculum of Identity

Prove or disprove the following 🏛 big idea:

> ### Attention getting AND giving are "personal."

Read biographies and autobiographies to validate or substantiate a 👓 perspective regarding the 🏛 big idea that is supported by ✿ details.

## LESSON D: STAYING ON TARGET

**PCM Focus:** Staying on target

**Objective:** Students will be able to recognize the importance of maintaining focus or "staying on the topic" when they phrase an idea in a discussion or present information to the class.

## MOTIVATE

Present students with the array of ideas and ask them to sort them into two groups that share common features.

Discuss the differences between the new groups that were formed: One group should contain related ideas, and the other should contain a set of disjointed ideas.

| | |
|---|---|
| The temperature rose to 100°. | She wore a coat. |
| It was summer. | It was February. |
| The dog barked. | It was a very hot day. |
| It was July 4th. | |

Discuss why the group that shares a theme for the same topic can be identified as "related, connected, or focused."

## ACTIVATE PRIOR KNOWLEDGE

Read the following scenarios to decipher the ramifications or consequences when students present an idea or communication that is not connected or is disjointed.

*Scenario 1:* I studied ants. They have three parts to their bodies. We have more parts to our body. We also have aunts. My aunt is Sally. Antennae are important to ants and their ability to taste and smell.

*Scenario 2:* I want to share what happened in the story. It was just like what happened to me when I baked cookies.

Discuss the following issues illustrating what happens when presentations are unfocused or digress from the topic:

- In what ways was the message clear or unclear?
- How was the message received by the listeners?
- How was the main idea the speaker wanted to share communicated effectively?
- How could the message be communicated in a clearer manner?

## RELATIONSHIP TO PCM

### Core Curriculum

Present the pictorial representation of a target. Discuss the importance of the "bull's eye" or center of the target in the game of archery.

 Discuss the parallels between a target and the delivery of a focused communication in a presentation.

Use the following target to guide the discussion.

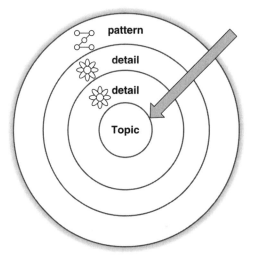

Apply the target chart to a presentation of a topic under study.

Use the following chart to guide a focused or "targeted discussion" about why "staying on topic" is a valued presentation skill when discussing each of the parallel curriculums.

| Curriculum of Practice | Curriculum of Connections | Curriculum of Identity |
|---|---|---|
| How does stating related ideas affect the understanding of a discipline? | How does staying on topic help to connect information? | How does staying on topic present the individual? |

# Appendix A

## Designing Curriculum Using the Parallel Curriculum Model

In the work represented in this text, the prevailing curricular rule has been to incorporate all four of the parallel curriculums in each of the lessons. Although all the authors of the parallel curriculum do not concur with this concept, using the four different types of parallel curriculum to form a single curricular structure provides students with opportunities to experience each of them with differing degrees of emphasis.

The majority of the lessons presented in the text comply with a distinctive order of presentation: Core Curriculum, Curriculum of Practice, Curriculum of Connections, and Curriculum of Identity. However, there are a variety of ways to organize and present the various parallel curriculums to create a curricular composition. The organization of the various parallels in a lesson or unit of study can be based on factors such as student interest, availability of resources, adherence to state or district standards, time constraints, and so on.

Following are some of the varied organizational structures that exemplify how the parallel curriculums could be ordered.

**Appendix A.1**

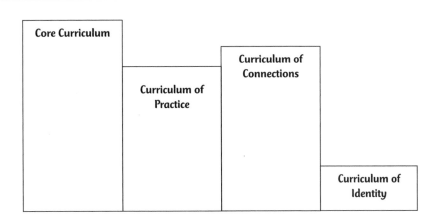

This configuration illustrates how both sequence and emphasis can be considered when presenting the parallel curriculum.

**Appendix A.2**

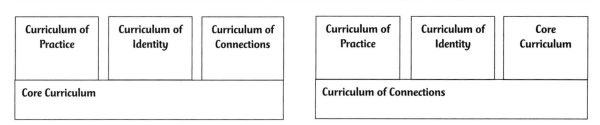

These configurations illustrate how one selected parallel curriculum forms the foundation upon which the other parallel curriculums are taught.

**Appendix A.3**

| Core Curriculum | Curriculum of Identity | Curriculum of Practice | Curriculum of Practice |
| --- | --- | --- | --- |
| **Juanita's Curriculum** | | | |

This configuration attempts to depict the ultimate means of utilizing the parallel curriculums. The structure allows the teacher and/or student to design the curriculum to meet individualized needs, interests, and abilities.

# Appendix B

## Teaching the Prompts of Depth and Complexity

Introducing students to the prompts of depth and complexity (pages 15–17) can be accomplished in many ways. Teaching the prompts is not as dependent on student readiness as much as on teacher determination. Teaching the prompts is also not dependent on learning the icons accompanying each of them. The icons were developed for two purposes: (1) to provide nonverbal representational cues for students and (2) to match the contemporary digital age where icons are frequently used to cue intellectual action. The prompts have been used successfully with students at all grade levels. These prompts represent the fundamental words that activate higher levels of knowing and were garnered from studies of expertise, Advanced Placement Free Response Questions, and various content taxonomies.

All skills need to be taught in stages: motivation, demonstration, application, and transfer. The prompts can be introduced and integrated into lessons as the basis of formulating questions or tasks:

*Question:* What is the ⬡ pattern that best describes the character's actions?

*Task:* Describe the character's ⬡ pattern of behavior.

*Question:* How do 📈 trends affect the development of inventions in our society?

*Task:* Identify the social and economic 📈 trends that promote inventiveness in our society.

Importantly, regardless of how the prompts are presented, they require instructional and intellectual rigor to become viable tools for students to use.

The prompts of depth and complexity can be introduced to students either formally or informally. An illustration of an informal means to develop an awareness of the prompts is to consistently make connections to the fact that students already know and use many of the prompts. For example, students can locate evidence of the prompt ⬡ *patterns* in the room as it is depicted in clothing, artwork, seating arrangements, and so on. Students can recall times when they were asked to state the *details* of a particular event. Basically, the prompts of depth and complexity are common terms students have acquired. The purpose of formalizing these prompts is to make them accessible and operational as a means to acquire and assimilate information.

Following is a lesson that integrates the teaching of the prompts of depth and complexity with the four parallel curriculums. This one lesson can be divided into a series of many lessons. Consider this lesson a way to prepare students for the more sophisticated lessons in the text.

# INTRODUCTION TO LEARNING THE PROMPTS OF DEPTH AND COMPLEXITY

## MOTIVATE

Discuss the many and varied ways people are prompted in the world of work, leisure, and entertainment. For example, people are prompted by signs such as these in the working world:

Notes and teleprompters in the entertainment field prompt people.

People are prompted by signs on the sidelines during a football game.

## ACTIVATE PRIOR KNOWLEDGE

Discuss the different types of keywords students have used in the various subject areas that assisted them to look for, recall, or make sense of what they learned. For example, keywords that aid in comprehending the meaning of a story include *who, when, where, why,* and *how.*

## RELATIONSHIP TO PCM

### Core Curriculum

Introduce the set of prompts related to depth that are connected to each other. For example, 👄 *language of the discipline,* ❀ *details,* ⚛ *patterns,* and ⬚ *trends* form a cluster that relate to and reinforce each other.

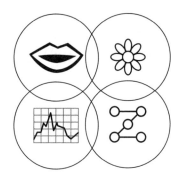

Introduce other prompts that are related or form sets: ⧗ *Patterns,* ⧉ *rules,* and ◆ *ethics* relate to each other. **?₂?** *Unanswered question* and ◆ *ethics* form a set.

Instruct students to apply these sets as sources to "dig or delve into" a body of knowledge. For example, How did the **?₂?** *unanswered questions* of the explorer's voyage create some ◆ *ethical issues* for the sailors?

## Curriculum of Practice

Facilitate students' understanding that different disciplines focus on different prompts for different purposes. Note the following examples:

| Discipline | Prompt | Purpose |
|---|---|---|
| Math | Patterns ⧗ | To determine the value |
| Science | Patterns ⧗ | To define properties |
| Language Arts | Patterns ⧗ | To detect genre |
| Social Studies | Patterns ⧗ | To identify the cause and effect |

## Curriculum of Connections

Select a particular prompt that can serve as a thread or organizer to provide cohesiveness to the curriculum. For example, students could be asked to relate the prompt 👓 *perceptions* within, between, and ⬠ *across disciplines.* This would be a means of addressing the impact each discipline has on the meaning and application of the same prompt 👓 *perceptions.*

## Curriculum of Identity

Apply the prompts to understanding self and others in interactions as students, family members, and friends. For example, students could discuss how the prompt ◯

*over time* affects relationships. Another example would be to ask students to debate the ◆ *ethics* of an issue they have confronted in fiction, real life, and so on.

Following are strategies to introduce, reinforce, and integrate the teaching and learning of the depth and complexity prompts into a lesson.

- Provide students with Post-Its to cue their understanding of a page of text in a new or more sophisticated manner. Instruct students to place the prompt on the Post-It to indicate how depth and/or complexity apply to the text.

- Develop a T-Square chart where students can make intersections between the prompts of depth and complexity to formulate questions or tasks.

What were the ◆ ethical issues that influenced 👓 perspectives?

- Provide open-ended learning strips that students can fill in with prompts of either depth or complexity or both to individualize their learning.

I will use _____ and _____ to study _____.

While studying _____, I will use _____ and _____.

- Present a target-like structure on a chart to focus attention on one or more prompts of depth and/or complexity as a catalyst for a discussion or debate.

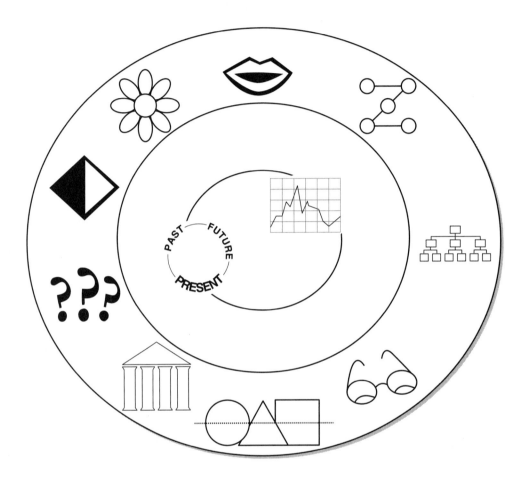

# References

Banks, J. A., & McGee Banks, C. A. (2003). *Multicultural education: Issues and perspectives* (4th ed.). New York: Wiley.

California Department of Education. (2001/2005). *Recommended standards for programs for gifted and talented students.* Sacramento, CA: Author.

California Department of Education and the California Association for the Gifted. (1994). *Differentiating the core curriculum and instruction to provide advanced learning opportunities.* Sacramento, CA: Author.

Good, T. L., & Brophy, J. E. (2008). *Looking in classrooms* (10th ed.). Boston: Allyn & Bacon, Pearson Education Inc.

Maslow, A. (1970). *Motivation and personality* (2nd ed.). New York: Harper & Row.

Moll, L. C., & Greenberg, J. B. (1990). Creating zones of possibilities: Combining social concepts for instruction. In L. C. Moll (Ed.), *Vygotsky and Education.* New York: Cambridge University Press.

Murrell, P. C. (2007). *Race, culture and schooling: Identities of achievement in multicultural urban schools.* New York: Lawrence Erlbaum Associates.

Pipher, M. (2002). *The middle of everywhere: The world's refugees come to our town.* New York: Harcourt Inc.

Project T.W.O. (1997). Jacob Javits Grant (R206A970006), University of Southern California.

Suarez-Orozco, C., Suarez-Orozco, M., & Todorova, I. (2008). *Learning a new land: Immigrant students in American society.* Cambridge, MA: The Belknap Press of Harvard University Press.

Tannenbaum, A. (1983). *Gifted children: Psychological and educational perspectives.* New York: Macmillan Publishing Co.

Tyler, R. (1949). *Basic principles of curriculum and instruction.* Chicago: University of Chicago Press.

# Index

**CORWIN**

A SAGE Company

The Corwin logo—a raven striding across an open book—represents the union of courage and learning. Corwin is committed to improving education for all learners by publishing books and other professional development resources for those serving the field of PreK–12 education. By providing practical, hands-on materials, Corwin continues to carry out the promise of its motto: **"Helping Educators Do Their Work Better."**